Praying from

the Free-Throw Line

—for Now

Praying from

the Free-Throw Line

—for Now

Minka Shura Sprague

A
JourneyBook
from
Church Publishing Incorporated New York

Library of Congress Cataloging-in-Publication Data

Sprague, Minka Shura.
    Praying from the free-throw line—for now / Minka Shura Sprague.
        p.   cm. — (JourneyBook)
    Includes bibliographical references (p.119).
    ISBN 0-89869-317-9 (pbk.)
    1. Meditations.   I. Title.   II. Series.
    BV4832.2S73   1999
    242—dc21
                                                            99-44125
                                                            CIP

JOURNEYBOOK and colophon are registered trademarks of Church Publishing Incorporated

Church Publishing Incorporated
445 Fifth Avenue
New York, NY 10016

5 4 3 2 1

for the memory of
Victor Judson Schramm
love
more than I could ask or imagine
. . . . .

WE WERE NOT YET unpacked from the move. I had resigned my position with the newspaper, kissed the community theater in beautiful downtown Hudson, Ohio, good-bye. The stuff of a village home was crammed into the apartment across from General Seminary in Chelsea on the West Side of New York City. August 1974: I had yet to begin seminary, the President of the United States had yet to resign from his office, I had found bunk beds for the kids. The journey had begun.

We were going to the grocery store. At the corner of Ninth Avenue and Twenty-second Street, I had the stroller in one hand, the kindergartner in the other. "I can cross the street by myself," he said. "I graduated from Traffic School."

"That was in Ohio," I said, hoping I sounded calm. All village children in Hudson had to graduate from Traffic School before attending their first year, whatever year that might be. He had done this in June before the move.

"Same red and green lights," he said. "I can do it by myself."

I took a deep breath, figuring it was now or later. I could not look at the oncoming traffic. I was honest with him; it had always been the best policy so far. "Okay," I said. "But I can't watch. I'll have to close my eyes. Can you do it by yourself that way?"

"Sure," he said.

When I had the courage to look, he was on the other side of Ninth Avenue, safe and sound. I count this as my first prayer from the free-throw line. A quarter of a century later: the kindergartner is a fine mathematician, the toddler has grown up to manage fashion, I am in the church. Who had a clue? These are some of the stories from the journey.

"Telling the stories?" The impishness in Bob's priestly face glowed. "Are you telling the one about the Key West bar?" he asked. "The one about your daughter on the Cathedral Close?"

· · · · · ·

"No way!" I shrieked. Not here. Those are simply outrageous stories. They tell God's outrageous love and divine-design, to be sure. But they are stories to tell in a good breeze. Ray Brown taught me a long time ago that there were stories to be told and stories to be written, that they were not necessarily the same ones. God rest his soul, he had a fine career as a New Testament scholar and a Roman Catholic clergyman. What was good enough for Ray Brown is good enough for me.

These are stories from the journey that tell of my finding of faith and love, my struggle to keep them both. "Surprised by joy," C. S. Lewis said, and I still am. I wasn't smart enough to pray for this life, am rarely smart enough to live it. When I do not have a clear task and/or a script, I automatically revert to feeling like Alice in Wonderland. I eat what people give me, go where people tell me, find myself in rituals I do not understand. By way of prayer, I seem to always find my way home.

The kindergartner crossed the street by himself. I unpacked the boxes and stuffed things in every corner of the apartment. Richard Nixon resigned as President of the United States. I began orientation.

I had been an Episcopalian half my life when I turned up for orientation. No one could have guessed this at the General Theological Seminary where everyone else seemed to have a vocation. I was the one who held up my hand and asked the New Testament professor to spell "eschatological." When a nice man told me he was the Suffragan Bishop, I actually told him I was sorry he wasn't feeling well.

Some orientation. I was asked what I thought about the Philadelphia Eleven.* "I have no idea," I blithely confessed. "Does Philadelphia have a new baseball team?" I was reminded,

---

* On July 29, 1974 eleven women were ordained priests at the Church of the Advocate in Philadelphia. These ordinations were widely criticized as irregular because the Episcopal Church had not yet authorized the ordination of women to the priesthood.

· · · · · ·

rather curtly, that baseball teams have only nine players. "I know that," I said indignantly. "My father played baseball." This, as it turns out, was just about all I knew. Some days, these days, this is still the case.

It turns out that I did not have to be smart to have this wonderful journey. I had to be faithful, any way I could do it. It was easier in the beginning when I was so naive—more, like Jesus says, "as a child." When I had spent all that wonderful naiveté, I had to learn some new moves for faith. Like "pick and roll," whatever this may actually mean basketball-wise. I'm still working at it.

On this journey of a quarter of a century, my blessings have been legion and I count them. All these words and stories are a long way to say so. The short form is this: the Bible is true, Jesus is real, God is faithful. There are free-throw lines everywhere for prayer; prayer works even when our eyes are closed.

Pentecost 1999

· · · · ·

BEING HUMAN, this is the way that it is: what is going on often does not match the way it feels. The right thing, divine-design-wise, may be going on and it feels awful. Indeed, we may do the right thing, whatever it is, and feel awful for days. This is normal for being human, knowing and feeling sometimes do not match.

When the reverse is true, doing the wrong thing divine-design-wise and it feels okay, we learn from it. This is generally called "making a mistake." Humans, like all animals, learn from making mistakes not to repeat them. But only humans, as far as I know, can do the right thing and feel awful about it for days.

Three days, in fact. I think of this as "It Takes Seventy-two Hours to Land." When I come home from travel, it takes me seventy-two hours to quit feeling lost in my own space. I call the island of Key West home and every time I claw my way there it takes me seventy-two hours to feel it, at home. When I've done the right thing and I feel awful afterwards, it takes the same time for me to land. I have learned that in seventy-two hours the guilt or remorse or dismay or whatever I feel will subside. Then, and only then, can I begin to think clearly.

Every time this happens, I have to remember that this is the way being human is. I have to pray more. I find myself apologizing to God for whining and picking at this feeling like a dog worrying a bone. Every time this happens, I take more showers than anyone who knows about ecology should take. I crave chocolate and fantasize that a glass of Merlot would be an antidote. I run until the sweat mandates I take the extra shower, no matter ecology. I go nuts inside. When I remember at last that this is just the way it is, the nuts-inside doesn't go away. Counting down the hours, however, helps me live. Seventy-two hours is the estimated time of arrival of my self.

· · · · · ·

While I count the hours, I also hold Jesus, John Lennon and a modified Malcolm X close. I try to be "wise as a serpent, gentle as a dove." I go for "whatever gets you through the night." I use nearly "any means necessary." I try to love me the way I believe God loves me. Not abusively.

Surely, it is divine-design that seventy-two hours is the time between Crucifixion and Resurrection. Life to death to life, this is, Crucifixion to Resurrection. Suddenly, I feel sheepish looking at my awful feelings compared to Jesus' incomparable ordeal. Well. This is human, too; embarrassing, to say the least. Embarrassing is the way being human is, too.

No wonder we sing Carl Daw's words to the tune of *Russia* at funerals. "Christ the Victorious, give to your servants / rest with your saints in the regions of light" is the right prayer for this life. "Grief and pain ended, sighing no longer" is our hope for whatever life after this life may bring.[*] In this life, we get embarrassing right along with grief and pain.

So did he, in this life, get grief and pain. His cry of abandonment from the cross is as humanly painful as it comes. Upon rising, was he embarrassed about all those "Are you sures?" in the garden? God knows. I know that the third time I asked my mother anything, she called it "nagging."

By the grace of God, we get it all: Jesus as brother and friend in this life; "grief and pain ended, sighing no longer" for the next one. Then, thank God, literally, we can expect an estimated time of arrival in seventy-two hours—three days.

---

[*] *The Hymnal 1982*, official hymnal of the Episcopal Church, #358.

. . . . . .

WHO IN THE WORLD would have supposed that I would grow up to teach Greek? Then, who could have guessed that Greek would be my guardian angel?

"Do you want to take Greek or Hebrew?" my advisor at the General Theological Seminary asked me in the late summer of 1974. I was on a Great Adventure. "Whatever you think," I said. He thought Greek. So I did.

"You are to assist Barbara in Greek; I think you are a teacher," my boss at General said in the late summer of 1978 or 1979. I was Assistant Director of Continuing Education, a low-level administrator. I had earned an M.A. in New Testament Studies, the prize for my Great Adventure. The thought of being a teacher had never once in my life entered my mind. "Whatever you think," I said. So I did.

"You are to take the Fellowship at General; this is right for you," said my friend Paul Gibson of the Anglican Church of Canada in the summer of 1980. I was terrified. Never mind that being a teacher had never entered my mind; "scholar" was unimaginable. I trusted Paul. "If you think so," I said. So I did.

"We need someone to teach Greek here so students can pass ordination exams; we think you can do this," said Bill Weisenbach of New York Theological Seminary in the summer of 1985 or 1986. "If you think so," I said. So I did.

A dozen or so years later, I think I have taught biblical Greek to people from every continent on the planet. At New York Theological Seminary, we offer Greek every year and there are usually thirty to forty people in the room on opening night. This class is often the best Off-Off-Off-Broadway show in town whenever it runs. The method developed by Barbara Hall provides the script. God does the choreography. I turn up as dance master.

. . . . . .

Over these years, astonishing things have happened in Greek class. One year, I lost a great love to spinal meningitis. One January, my mother died the weekend before classes were to begin. One summer, the police arrived on the first night of class. Regularly, someone brings a guest to the show. Regularly, personal stories I never expect to tell in public fly out of my mouth. No one has ever ever failed this course. Everyone always does better than they expect to do. "If you think so," I say to the Almighty. So we do.

Over these years, Greek itself has saved my life. While my great love let go of his life in an intensive care unit, I held still by diagramming verses from 2 Corinthians. When I could not imagine a world without my mother nearby, I taught participles. When I have needed Jesus and his words, they've been there. In Greek. In Greek, the word for angel can mean message or messenger. Both of these, Greek has been for me.

On my computer Scrabble game, Greek counts as a word meaning "don't know." Knowing that Greek is my guardian angel, I think this is fair, too. My whole life has been "Greek to me," according to this definition. I had no idea about this life. Who knew?

The author of Hebrews knew that we don't know. The safeguard is hospitality; "thereby some have entertained angels unawares." (Hebrews 13:2, RSV) Advisors on Great Adventures, employers, friends—all these turned out to have been angels. I seem to have entertained them unawares.

Message, messenger. Aware, unaware. My life is still a surprise—"Greek"—to me. That Greek is my guardian angel, of this I am certain. Unawares, too.

. . . . . .

GOD KNOWS what the diversity at New York Theological Seminary will bring. I've learned this in the classroom, at the faculty table, in community gatherings. Even sitting quietly at my desk with only a concordance for company.

We are insistently interdenominational and multicultural here. This is true in the classroom, at the faculty table, in community gatherings. When it looks—in any of these places—like we might be missing a language or a gender or a flavor of Christianity we can ask or imagine, we go looking for it.

I love this. I learn God's world in this mix. I learn myself in this mix—as woman, as teacher, as Episcopalian, as deacon. The joy of finding commonality in difference is tremendous. Knowing that God will do the choreography among us, having called us all forth, is a relief. Recognition of one's particularity is reassuring.

Daily, I can be surprised by the way this mix shakes out in the moment. Sometimes the surprises are delightful. Sometimes, the surprises are appalling. Sometimes, it is just the way it is, God knows.

Intentional diversity takes time and awareness. Assumptions can cause disasters. All these cultures and languages and pieties lurk beneath the surfaces of our conversations, our decisions. Centuries of injustice can threaten generosity at any moment. Misunderstanding is always possible.

Once in a while, misunderstanding brings laughter, God knows.

"God knows," I said in a faculty meeting when resolution on some issue was impossible. "Are we agreed about this?" We were. Would we postpone discussion on this issue to a later date? We would.

· · · · · ·

Weeks went by. Professor Han, my colleague in the biblical field, stopped by my office to ask what we had done about this issue. "Nothing," I said. "We put it under 'God knows.'"

"Yes," he said, "I remember. But what did we do about it?"

"Nothing," I said. "That's why we called it 'God knows.'"

"Yes," he said. There was a pause. He looked at me with puzzlement between his eyebrows. "What do you think it means when you say, 'God knows'?"

"Ah," I said. "'God knows' means nobody knows."

"Ah," Han said. "To your people. To my people, 'God knows' means everybody knows. That's why I thought something had happened, that I was the only one who didn't know."

"Oh no," I said. "When I said 'God knows' I meant I didn't know. That's why I put it under old business and 'God knows.'"

"So who knows? No one knows?" he asked, mischief instead of puzzlement now all over his face.

"Han, please," I said, and we both collapsed in laughter.

I think my understanding of "God knows" comes from an old German expression: "Who knows? God knows." Did this expression come to the United States through Ellis Island like so many other customs and cultures? God knows. This means I don't know. So how is it that in Korea, "God knows" means that everybody knows?

Who cares? God must, I think, or we wouldn't all be here in this mix together. Me, too. I'm grateful for it, God knows.

I WALKED TOWARD this computer life slowly. Lots of friends and colleagues urged me to purchase a machine. Right now. As soon as possible. Some of these friends and colleagues went on to ridicule relentlessly the antiquated word processor that served me well. I finally called Arthur, my friend Laurie's husband. Arthur had done business on several continents, surely he could help. He could. It was Arthur who said, "Don't even think about this until you know exactly why you need it."

Then he taught me how to do the banking. "Every month," he said, "put $250 in a savings account in your mind. You are saving this much money every month, in terms of the industry, by waiting until you know. When you have about $2,500 saved, you will know or you will know that you don't know. If you know exactly why you need it, it ought to cost you just about this much. If you know that you don't need it, you will have enough money in your mind to take a great trip—like to Maui."

I did this. I knew I did not know exactly why I needed a computer. I also knew that Arthur counts as an expert in matters of money and Maui.

One morning, I sat up in bed and knew exactly why I needed a computer. I had been given permission to rewrite the Greek grammar I use in seminary. Sweet antiquated word processors do not do Greek. I checked my mental savings account. I had exactly $2,500 in my mind. "So much for Maui," I thought rather sadly as I made my way to coffee.

Arthur was right on both counts: he knew that I would know exactly; my first computer cost "about $2,500." I was ready to do this.

Being ready and getting it done, however, turned out to be different ball games. It was hard to spend my mental savings. I had all this money in my mind and I had to let it go.

Then, please, I had to go the store. Then, I had to pick something out. When push came to shove, I had to take friends with me.

But, I did it. I got the computer into the house. I figured out how to open it. Day by day, I began to learn its ways, not my ways. Anxiety dreams began to litter my sleep. In these dreams, I was always inadequate—in classrooms, in liturgy, in supermarkets and airports and at family gatherings. In the sixth or seventh one of these awful dreams, I turned to my daughter and said, "All habits can change." I sat up in bed the next morning and knew I would be all right.

So I am, all right. The Greek grammar is long since written. I am on the next computer. In the meantime, I have learned a lot about how hard it is to spend freely. I have to spend enormous effort to remember that I am called to spend my life—all my resources, my very breath as well as time and money. "This is the moment you have," I must say to my self. "This is your life. The cross of Christ has already saved your life; you are to spend it." I must continually remind myself that I am to spend my life for love.

I hold Arthur close here, too. I have seen him spend his money, his time, his life for love. I know how tiny Hana—named for the love of Maui—stretched her way into his arms for life, for love. I have something of an idea of what Arthur had to spend for love of this child.

It takes faith to spend my life freely. Faith that resources called to be spent will be there again when I need them. Faith that God, who has provided until now, will do so in the future. It also takes faith to wait until I know exactly where and how and why I need to spend. Whatever. Except my breath for life and love.

The Question

· · · · ·

IN MY MEMORY, February 2 is always on the calendar in the General Theological Seminary catalogue. Along with Christmas, Easter, and Michaelmas, February 2 is a high holy day. This is the day, on the calendar in the GTS catalogue, Th.D. dissertations are submitted.

Once I asked how often this high holy day had been observed. "Not often," the glare that met me suggested. Rising midnight on February 1, 1985, however, I was about to keep this high holy day myself. Expecting nothing less than lightning to strike, I was typing footnotes for the Th.D. dissertation I was to walk down the steps the next day.

It was pretty late for my twelve-year-old to be up. Much less, sitting on the edge of my bed. "Mom, I have just one question," she said. Who knew this was the lightning about to strike?

"Honey, why aren't you asleep?" I asked. Then, just in case she hadn't noticed, "I'm pretty busy."

"I can't sleep," she said. "I need to ask you just one question."

I actually considered telling her how many times I had seen February 2 go by unobserved. How this was a high holy day. How I suspected lightning would strike, I was so close to keeping it. She's not going to care, I thought, she's twelve. "Are you sure it can't wait until morning?" I asked.

"I'm sure."

"Okay," I said with resignation and a smile. "What's the one question?"

"Were you a virgin when you married my dad?"

Lightning by any other name. I looked out the window, took a breath. "Help!" I said silently to the Almighty. I took another breath. Then, I heard me say, "Sweetheart, there are two answers to this question. Yes or no. Are you prepared to take either answer to this question?" And then silently to the Almighty, "Thank you."

· · · · · ·

"Yes," she said.

"Yes or no?" I asked.

"Yes."

"No."

She was devastated. She cried out loud and jumped up and down and all but tore her hair like one observing ancient Greek mourning rites. I watched.

"One more," she finally said.

"One more what?" I asked.

"One more question."

"Okay," I said. Where I grew up, lightning rarely strikes in the same place twice.

"You only did it once before you married my dad, right? Just once?"

"Sweetheart," I said, going for the same answer to prayer. "There are two answers to this question, yes or no. Are you prepared to accept either one as the answer? Yes or no?"

"Yes."

"No."

Well. What goes around, comes around, as they say. I must confess that I knew something of this in the 60s when this stage, so to speak, was set. This was long before I knew how to say, "This is a universe in which nothing is wasted, nothing is lost" and call it good news no matter how it feels. But even then, I knew about consequences. Rising midnight of the high holy day of my Th.D. dissertation, I knew this was all in the design.

Oikonomia is the New Testament's name for this design, God's design. This is more than "plan" as we get it in recent English translations of Ephesians 1:10. This is deep structure—architecture and choreography combined—God's divine-design. In this *oikonomia*, divine-design, nothing is wasted or lost, energy moves into matter and back again, earth herself is a recycled star. Of course, what goes around, comes around.

· · · · · ·

Nothing is left out of what goes around, comes around. A variety of old debts can turn up here. So do second chances of all sorts, right alongside lightning strike questions before midnight. Decades later, my oldest college friend found me. Under palm trees, we laughed until it hurt as she described how demolished I was the first time I fell in love. "I lost most of my sophomore year," I confessed. "And I had to repeat astronomy. But wait until you hear how this came down on the Th.D. high holy day. It was *the* question."

"THERE ARE TWO WAYS to raise children," Deena said with certainty. "You can say "yes" unless there's a good reason to say "no." Or, you can say "no" unless there is a good reason to say "yes." Deena and I were both mothers and students at General Seminary. As soon as she said it, my whole life sorted right before my eyes.

I cannot recall the conversation nor the issue that occasioned the pronouncement. I can pinpoint the year. Easter dinner that year is etched forever on my soul. It was a direct result.

The minute the words were out of her mouth, I knew she was right. I also knew that I wanted to say "yes" unless there was a good reason to say "no" and not the other way around. Mentally, I did an inventory, took the score. I was about fifty-fifty, just this edge of appalled.

I must have stayed in the rest of this conversation. Surely, I got the breakfasts and lunches made, all of us to school et cetera in the days that followed. All I remember is walking my life with Deena's words on my mind. How could it be that I was fifty-fifty here? Why in the world would I prohibit my children without a good reason? Anyone? Myself? Saying "no" unless there was a good reason to say "yes" struck me as living negatively. Worse, it seemed like asking the universe to prove itself with every step.

One day I could see my patterns. When I was rested and centered and secure, I said "yes" unless there was a good reason to say "no" on a dime. To the kids, the universe, myself, I did this instinctively. When I was tired, overwhelmed, interrupted or fearful in any way, I tended to say "no" unless there was a good reason to say "yes." I also seemed to do this instinctively, on a dime.

I started watching myself. I slowed down when choices arrived or the kids asked me to make them. I wanted to live with "yes." I didn't want to miss a blessing, miss offering one. I began to hear myself say things like, "I don't know. I'm busy right now. Can we decide this

. . . . . .

after dinner?" When my son said something about "putting things off," I sat him and his sister down and told them what Deena had said, what I was doing. He was twelve, my daughter was nine and they got it. On a dime.

Watching myself became my Lenten discipline. Never has Lenten observance been so satisfying. When I took inventory, my average was going up and up. Easter was coming, too. Nice.

Schedules were complex in our house, particularly at holidays. There would be no food in the house on the day of Resurrection if I didn't get the shopping done early. "So, what do we want for Easter dinner?" I asked one evening.

"Tacos!!!" they said in unison. Then, in stereo, "What's the good reason to say 'no'?" On a dime.

I made the nine-year-old go with me to the supermarket. There was no way I was going to endure this alone. Our cart was overflowing when we got to check-out: refried beans, ground beef, cheese, tomatoes, onions, tortillas, avocados. I looked around at other carts: roasts of beef, pork loins, legs of lamb. I yearned for sunglasses.

Mutely, I watched the woman who always totaled my groceries ring up our order. I avoided her eyes. Then I had to pay. "So," she said with a huge grin, "didn't anybody tell you it's Easter?"

I looked at the nine-year-old with "your turn" on my face. She was perfect. "There wasn't a good reason to say 'no'," she fairly chirped. "And Kathryn is bringing the margarita pie for dessert!"

"It's a long story," I said to the cashier's quizzical look. "Have a great Easter."

It was a great Easter dinner. Saying "yes" unless there's a good reason to say "no" has given us all a great Easter life, a Resurrection life. There is a growing list of things to which I now say "no," but I can tell you exactly how I got there. Margarita pie is not on this list. I would say "yes" to margarita pie again, on a dime.

. . . . . .

I HAVE LEARNED to argue myself backwards for certainty and courage. This may be the other side of the coin for saying "yes" unless there is a good reason to say "no." When I can't quite say "yes" and do not know the good reason to say "no," I come at myself from the other direction. "Do I have any reason to think I will regret not doing this?" I ask. If the answer is in any way "yes," I can usually find the reasons for suspecting I might regret not going ahead. These reasons almost always come down to "I will never know unless I try."

I learned the line and the logic when I was confronted with my twenty-fifth high school reunion. My girlfriends from beautiful downtown Liberty, Missouri, chased me down in New York City. As wonderful as it was to be with women I had known since third grade, I was hesitant to return. I had not set foot in that town for a quarter of a century. Should I? Shouldn't I? When I finally had the sense to pray about it, the question came, followed by the answer—I did have reasons to suspect I would regret not returning home for such an occasion.

One high school reunion in Liberty will do me for a lifetime. I had good reasons to say "no" when the thirtieth came around. The reasons I had left that town the minute I graduated from high school were all still there. It still felt small and a little mean, like someone might ask me, "And who were her mother's people?" Then, aside from my wonderful girlfriends, I felt like the only person not from the movie *Peggy Sue Got Married*. But I would not have missed my twenty-fifth reunion for the world. There was even an unexpected party favor: it turned out that I had a leftover romance from the seventh grade ripe for consummation.

By the time Laurie said, "Let's go to Hazor and dig," I had become good at this analysis. Did I have any reason to suspect I might regret not having my hands in soil older than all of Judaism and Christianity? Did I suspect that I would never know unless I tried? Oh, yes.

· · · · · ·

This was enough to put me on Mount Canaan with a pickax and a spoon.

One foray into archeology will do me for a lifetime. "You're on your own," I said to Laurie when the second summer rolled around. This was not my field and I could feel this every minute of every day. Furthermore, the communal living felt like church camp and I am long past being real happy about months and months of church camp. But I would not have known this without trying. And there was an unexpected party favor in Israel, too. I had a little bit of time in Tel Aviv and actually sat for coffee and conversation on Ben Yehudah Street, following in the footsteps of Oskar Schindler.

One day I confessed to my youngest sister that I had to do this, come around backwards to give myself certainty and courage. "This is my safeguard for regret," I said. "I would rather risk making mistakes than miss my life."

"Dad says the same thing," she said. "This is advice he gave me years ago. He says it's not what you have done that you will regret later; it's what you haven't done."

"What do you suppose that could possibly be?" I asked her and we both laughed.

We think he's done just about everything. Furthermore, I'm hoping that when I am his age, the party favor is that people say the same for me.

. . . . . .

HE COULD NOT RESIST. He had to open the door, insert himself into the classroom, tell us he loved us. He knew this was a class on "Scripture and Violence." He knew that there were only six of us, that we were all women. He had to interrupt. He could not resist.

This was the whole point of this course on "Scripture and Violence"—to examine violence in the Bible and violence in our lives. Not being able to resist is at the heart of violence. Where God does not resist anger, where parents and other caretakers do not resist abuse, where lovers do not resist and love-making becomes rape. "He could not resist" could have been the subtitle of this course.

Not a single man registered for this course. Only as many women as the fingers on a hand turned up. This course was linked to conferences, congregational issues, prestigious grant money. But when push came to shove, no one wanted to take it. When push comes to shove—this, too, was the point of this course—no one wants to take violence.

The course began with Genesis 2:4–3:24. We all begin here, the story in which the woman cannot resist, the man cannot resist, God cannot resist. This is the story that sets humanity on its way. Male and female, together making one image of God, we are sent out of the garden with God's anger at our back. It is a terrible way to begin. We talked it out.

We talked him out, too. He illustrated the whole point of the course when he opened the classroom door, inserted himself into the room. He was uninvited. He crossed someone else's boundary. He turned push into shove. He claimed what was not his own. Could we call this violence? Yes. We decided, however, that we knew his intentions, his love. We decided that knowing him allowed us to trust his love, even when it was offered uninvited. There was, we agreed, tension between the form of the act and the content of the love.

· · · · · ·

The truth of our human existence lies in this tension. There is inherent and potential violence at the heart of all human ways. For these ways, we have Genesis for a beginning, the cross of Christ for a beginning of the end. Genesis insists that we remember that all our relationships can become an awful beginning. Jesus' willing death, we Christians claim, is where the walk out of the garden ends. Beyond anger, God will raise this child, pour out Holy Breath on all humanity in Jesus' name. In the light of the Resurrection and the outpouring of the Holy Spirit, we are forever forgiven.

"Now we see by way of a mirror, enigmatically; then we shall see face to face," says the Apostle Paul. "Now I know in part; then I shall recognize even as I am recognized. Now faith, hope, love occupy, these three. And the greatest of these is love." (1 Corinthians 13:12–13)

The knowing, even partially, matters. Seeing, even partially, matters. When love occupies the act—even an invasive act—seeing and knowing allow the love to be made known. He could not resist; we recognized his love.

With forgiveness instead of anger at our back, we are offered this walk as a way. We are not to forget the inherent violence. We are to know it and to name it. We are to recognize its potential in ourselves and others. We are also to accept forgiveness, allow faith, hope and love to occupy our bodies, hearts and souls.

When love occupies, we grow beyond vulnerability. We become transformed. However human, however inherently violent, we become generous enough to recognize each other, our intentions. Receiving forgiveness for ourselves, we receive others. We, too, become unable to resist. We make it, unable to resist, love.

. . . . . .

I'M LOOKING AT LATITUDES on a map of the world. On this map, my world is carved into areas called "nations." I look at the circles called latitudes cutting through it all and think about how "nations" come and go. How peoples come and go. Sometimes we remember them. Sometimes, when peoples go, they are lost forever.

I come and go between two latitudes these days—latitude 40° when I am in Manhattan in New York City, latitude 24° when I am in Key West. On my map, I can move westerly across latitude 40° and think I know something about the other peoples with whom I share this space—in Indiana, Missouri and northern California, for instance. Moving easterly, it is harder. I know I barely know about peoples in Madrid, Rome, Istanbul and Tashkent.

Of latitude 24°, in either direction, I know nothing. Westerly is deep in Mexico; easterly is through southern Algeria, touching the Nile south of Egypt, through Oman and north of Bombay. Oh, my.

All I know about these latitudes is a little about the weather. This isn't much. Can I assume that the seasons come and go in Istanbul as they do in New York? I'd be surprised if southern Algeria has a hurricane season like Key West. And what about the peoples that have come and gone?

I actually teach a "civilization," a collection of peoples that have come and gone: the Roman Empire, the culture and society in which Jesus lived and walked. The face of this civilization changes from time to time, province to province as the literature we call the New Testament emerges. I've taught this for years. I've never looked at the rise of Christianity by way of latitudes. I wonder if this would make a difference.

Thinking about the world in terms of latitudes is a "global" way to think of the peoples who are present on the planet earth. Increasingly, we—the peoples of the planet earth—are

· · · · · ·

beginning to think beyond nations for justice and environmental global realities.

I am a child born of the Second World War. The peoples of the world at the time of my birth thought globally in terms of race, religion and empire. Six million Jews alone died in this war, all of them related to Jesus, Christian cousins. I feel slaughter as I look at latitudes and think of global realities. I would rather the peoples of my world relate to one another according to latitude rather than race, religion, or empire. I look at latitudes and dream of a day beyond nations.

I do not expect a day beyond nations to come soon. I do meditate on latitudes, however. I walk these words by Barry Lopez in prayer for a healthy planet, peoples who find each other across latitudes for love.

Once in your life you ought to concentrate your mind
upon the remembered earth. You ought to give yourself
up to a particular landscape in your experience;
to look at it from as many angles as you can,
to wonder upon it, to dwell upon it.
You ought to imagine
that you touch it with your hands at every season
and listen to the sounds that are made upon it.

You ought to imagine
the creatures there
and all the faintest motions of the wind.
You ought to recollect the glare of the moon
and the colors of the dawn and dusk.*

---

* Barry Lopez, *Arctic Dreams*, Bantam Books,Inc.,NY, 1986. Frontispiece.

. . . . . .

My daughter Caroline was six years old, had a friend over to play. We were living in Brooklyn Heights in the late 70s, winters filled with snow. "What is incarnation?" I overheard the friend ask.

"That milk that comes in a box," Caroline said. "The thin kind. You mix it. You know, when there's too much snow. When the trucks can't get milk to Brooklyn."

Later, it happened that these snowy Brooklyn winters were a Manhattan intermission. I had come to the General Theological Seminary with the kids in the mid-70s, did the M.A. in Chelsea. After the three snowy Brooklyn winters, we would return to General Theological Seminary for half of the next decade. Caroline arrived at seminary in a stroller. She was eligible for a bat mitzvah when we left. "Incarnation is that milk that comes in a box" tells it true: children who are raised in seminary become theologians, no matter what.

I look up the definitions—she was not so far off. To be incarnate, Webster says, is to be invested with bodily form, to be made manifest. So water makes milk, incarnates the crystals when there is too much snow for the trucks to come to Brooklyn. Water, mixed with "Carnation" powder, actualizes milk. Thin milk, yes. Milk, nevertheless.

The Incarnation, Christians name the union of human and divine in Jesus, Risen Christ. Jesus is the incarnation of God in bodily form, God made manifest. The divine in concrete, actual form. Human and divine are somehow mixed. The Gospel of John describes the process: "The Word became flesh and dwelt among us." (John 1:14)

We, on the other hand, celebrate our own incarnate lives through the death and resurrection of this one. Already flesh, we become Word by way of Spirit, through baptism. Our bodily forms become God made manifest. Signed and sealed as Christ's own forever, Holy Breath mingles with our own. Our inhalations and exhalations actualize Holy Spirit, Holy Breath.

Next to Jesus, our incarnations pale. The Incarnation is fully divine as well as human, we are not. What Jesus does perfectly, we will always do imperfectly. Jesus is our promise and our hope, our way for the walk. We can never fully walk his way. The Incarnation is rich whole milk, we are thin milk. Milk, nevertheless.

Years later, we were in Yorkville, uptown in Manhattan, near Gracie Mansion and the East River. Caroline's eligibility for bat mitzvah and the snowy Brooklyn winters had come and gone. She and a friend passed through my Bible-littered work space. The friend took a long look. "Is your mom religious?" she asked.

Caroline thought carefully as they turned the corner of the living room. "No," she said. "She's faithful."

It was all I could do to sit still. I wanted to jump up and down and shout "Alleluia!" I wanted to lean out my windows and tell all the world how wonderful and smart she was. I wanted the distinction engraved on every clerical collar for the world to see: "You may think I'm religious; really, I'm faithful. My daughter tells me so."

I resisted. I didn't say a word aloud. I let them pass and thanked God with every red corpuscle in my bloodstream for the moment, praying I would be steward of such a distinction. For the moment, all of the "Am I scarring these kids forever?" vanished from my mind. I trusted the Incarnation. This moment, I even trusted my own thin milk incarnation.

Milk, nevertheless. I love it. Manifestly.

. . . . . .

WE ALL GET in by adoption. Paul is very clear about this in Galatians 3:23–4:7. In the late 50s of the first century in the Roman Empire, this made perfect sense. Children by blood lived next to children by adoption everywhere, inherited their fathers' estates equally.

This is how you can see what God has done in the life and death and Resurrection of Jesus Christ, Paul says, "now that faith has come." By faith and by the power of God's Holy Spirit we all get in by adoption. Paul is translating the cross, saying what it means in the language of his world. Children by blood, children by Holy Spirit, Holy Breath. "If a son," he says in the language of those who mostly inherit in the first century Roman Empire, "then an heir."

I first saw this clearly over a cappuccino at the Cornelia Street Cafe. Laurie and I had yet again turned up to sort out our lives over cappuccinos. We had found each other in a Hebrew class and had done this ever since. This time, she and Art were beginning to take the steps that would call in, by adoption, wonderful lives from around the world. We were, of course, talking about all the problems people always mention when adoption is discussed. I opened my mouth, heard Paul come out of it. "We all get in by adoption," I heard me say. "This is Galatians. He says this is what God does. He assumes it works."

I needed to know more. I read and read, realizing that adoption was more than tolerated in the Empire. Adoption advanced the Empire's boundaries. The problems people always mention when adoption is discussed were discussed then, too. But also discussed was how adoption diffused and broadened cultural identities, how wonderful this was. I began to see adoption and Christianity differently. I began to think of adoption as what God did. If adoption had worked for us all, for upwards of a hundred generations, surely we could expect it to work now.

· · · · · ·

I watched adoption work for Laurie and Art. Neoma came from Korea, Hana came from China. I learned the miraculous adventure and resilience already so obvious in the lives of these little ones. Then, Malcolm came from Korea. By this time, I had stretched my thinking from the Roman Empire to the Milky Way and beyond. Beyond broadening culture and boundaries, never mind the Roman Empire and the United States of America, I began to envision divine-design beyond the stars. Now Maile has come from China, too. These are only the two-footed creatures that have found their way from beyond the stars to be this family. I cannot count the four-footed ones—horses, dogs, cats—who have come to belong by adoption as well.

Good enough for the Roman Empire, belonging by adoption is good enough for me. When the church was legal and powerful and running the world in what we call the Middle Ages, it was not good enough for the church—not for inheritance, that is. The church made inheritance by adoption illegal in these years. The church did not want her cultural identity diffused. She chose not to be broadened by boundaries advanced by adoptive children. Were there no children by blood, the church got the land.

Oh how paltry Laurie's and my conversations over cappuccino these days would be were this still the case. Never mind the stories from school, the foals to come, our own stories of struggle to become ourselves. Had not Paul translated the cross by way of adoption, what language would I use for my faith?

We all inherit by Holy Breath. Holy Spirit, Holy Breath, Holy Wind: these all translate the Greek *hagia pneuma*. We could even say, in the language of classic films, we all *Inherit the Wind*.

. . . . . .

THE KIDS ON THEIR OWN, I moved onto a sleepy street in Manhattan with long-abandoned stables. Martin, a nice man, originally from Ireland, opened the bar and restaurant around the corner soon after. I became a neighbor, a brunch and ball game regular.

The sleepy and the stables have disappeared. Martin's staff has changed. Nipper, for instance, has gone on to pizza on other shores and Natalie has a baby. I've changed, too. I am still a neighbor, a brunch and ball game regular. I make pilgrimage around the corner for what I think is the best French toast on the island. I count sunny brunch in the garden a trip to the beach. I perch on stools for playoffs.

My favorite regulars are a couple in this garden. He has white bushy hair that looks passionate. She basks in the sun in an elastic tube top. She is garrulous, will have endless and absorbing conversations with strangers at nearby tables. I don't sit nearby, ever. These conversations drift in and out of my awareness. "That was fun!" she exclaimed one Saturday to him, after the departure of the man at the next table. "That was Mr. Cell Phone. He's so smart."

Am I Ms. French Toast? I turn magazine pages and wonder. I think about what I know here and what I do not know. I think about how much I cherish the public, the anonymous, the neighborliness of it all.

I do not know their names. Are they married? What does she do? From the conversations I overhear, all these are possible: the New York Historical Society; director of an art gallery; film critic; political organizer. What I do know is that she is at home here—in the garden, in her body.

My world would be so much less without them, I think. My world would be less without Martin's around the corner. Here, I am neighbor and proximity is my role, not teacher,

· · · · · ·

mother, sister, deacon. The clothes I wear here do not matter. I tend to wear some. But I could take most of them off the way she does and it would be fine.

This is being neighbor a different way than it happens in the story of the Good Samaritan. In Luke 10:29–37, the point is responsibility, who steps up in crisis on the road to Jericho. Being neighbor at Martin's is the other side of the coin, inclusion with anonymity. Martin's is something of a road to Jericho without crisis.

My world would be so much less without my roles—teacher, mother, sister, deacon. These roles are my privilege for life and love. In these roles, however, the clothes often matter. More than this, my functioning in these roles allows others to have expectations of me, even reasonable ones. I balance my life in these roles by being an anonymous neighbor around the corner at Martin's.

I had been going to Martin's about a year when one day I knew I needed to tell them what I did for a living. I had had the whole year off, had loved every anonymous minute. Driven by intuition and fueled with Cobb salad, I thanked them for their friendship. Then I put all the truth on the bar: deacon, the cathedral, the seminary. "I need for you to know this," I said. "You have been so good to me."

One week later, I was the preacher for a service out on Long Island. From the pulpit, I saw someone from Martin's, right there in congregation. Indeed, he and I had been at each other's throats all through the Knicks' playoffs. Anonymously. At the reception, he was all smiles, like he had just discovered something.

Me, too, all smiles on the train. On this road to Jericho, I was first.

"And who is my neighbor?" Someone, around every corner. It bears watching.

MADISON SQUARE IS MY PARK, my little piece of paradise. I share it with everyone in the world and then some. Dogs, lovers, homeless people are always there. During the work week, lovers mingle with business lunchers. After this, the variety seems endless. Rallies of all sorts, even Albanian-Americans. Bagpipers, Shakespearean actors. One Sunday afternoon, a pair of men's underpants hung on the fence to dry for all the world to see. Jockey shorts, not boxers.

All the statues in Madison Square face south, downtown. When Admiral Farragut was sculpted here, he surveyed all the action. A century ago, shopping was below Twenty-third Street. Women socialized at the Square by horse and carriage. Between 1876 and its placement in the bay, the Statue of Liberty's hand and torch made a visit. For a nickel, you could climb and see far more than the Admiral.

Madison Square fits the ancient definition of paradise—an enclosed park or pleasure-ground. The Persians coined the term and we have record of it since the fourth century B.C.E. It could be that Persian kings and nobles socialized in paradise just like New York City women in the nineteenth century.

The word paradise occurs in the New Testament only three times. Paul says, "I know that this man was caught up into Paradise." (2 Corinthians 12:4) The Spirit speaks in Revelation 2:7: "To the one who conquers I will grant to eat of the tree of life, which is the paradise of God." The paradise with which we are most familiar is Luke 23:43, Good Friday fare. The word is on Jesus' lips; Jesus' body is on the cross. "Today," he promises the criminal beside him, "you will be with me in Paradise."

The promise to the criminal is made in dying. In rising, the promise holds good for all of us. In dying, we share the promise made to the criminal outside Jerusalem that day.

· · · · · ·

Because we live in the rising, we get it today, too. We get to be with him in paradise. Wherever that may be, today.

Madison Square is my regular little piece of this paradise. Late summer roses give way to stark trees, squirrels scurry, dogs run. Snow covers, leaves bud. I go to this piece of paradise for solace, for sun, to hold still in turmoil. I count on the promise that he is with me here. Whenever.

I have begun to watch others in their little pieces of paradise. I particularly like the Bellevue South Park, the collection of Spanish-speaking men for whom this park seems to be paradise. They congregate here in season and out of season. They share meals and drinks, play cards and dominos. Sometimes they even decorate, drape banners in the trees. I am regular enough, passing through this paradise as I run, to get smiling greetings.

There are no statues the likes of Admiral Farragut in the Bellevue South Park. In one direction, willow trees flank great playground equipment and a basketball court. In the other direction, Bellevue Hospital looms. This big, bustling general hospital holds the psychiatric ward made famous by the movies. There is a jail ward, too. Criminals, like the one Jesus promised as he was dying, are here.

This strikes me as divine architecture, just right. Everything is here. I can see it all as I run through Bellevue South Park. The criminal's entreaty; the promise. All kinds of us as we are in the world: the gatherers, the ill, the shoppers, the criminals, the runners who pass through. In dying—and we all are—we get the promise. The promise of paradise is ours for today, too, if we can see it. Anywhere. The criminal's entreaty of Jesus is our reward. He is with us, in this paradise. Just like he promised. Today.

. . . . . .

I AM AT A GREAT BIRTHDAY PARTY with friends and strangers in Greenwich Village. Toward the close of the evening, one of these strangers says, "Please let me walk you home. I've heard stories about you for years. I have a million questions to ask you."

"Sure," I reply. Stories of people I have heard about for years leap into my mind like Moses' frogs in the land of Egypt. Should I turn up at a birthday party with these people, I would do the same. I would ask if I could ask. This wonderful woman has just taught me the way to do it.

We step out onto Waverly Place and she begins to ask. How was it for women in the Episcopal Church in the late 70s? Who was ordained to the priesthood, who was not, how it did all happen? It's a sweet walk. Did you really do this, say this, did this really happen?

I am thinking that I love the way stories bind us as the Body of Christ. So it is we tell how God sent the frogs to plague Pharaoh in the land of Egypt. How Jesus said this or that by the Sea of Galilee. How Margaret Mead told the Episcopal bishops we needed the Noah story for baptism. Good heavens, even me, how I did indeed say this or that. I am reminded that creation does not keep secrets; only people do. How "public" our lives really are. I'm thinking that I rather wish some of these things had gone unsaid. I'm worrying, here and there, about what else people have said about me. We turn up Broadway.

"Okay," I say, "what's next?"

She stops in front of Paragon Sporting Goods. "I only have one more," she says. "I can't believe I'm going to ask it."

"Okay," I say, "What is it?"

She shakes her head, laughs. I tell her about teaching church camp, the kinds of questions teenagers ask when you say you will answer any question. I tell her that only God and the answers to my prayers shock me these days.

"Okay," she says. "Are you rich?"

I laugh so hard I suspect the skis and golf clubs fall off their racks inside the store. Broadway is warm and empty, my laughter bounces off the buildings. She has caught me totally by surprise.

Finally, I recover. "Do people say I am rich?" I ask.

"Yes," she says, "they do."

"Well," I say. The stars come closer as I take a breath. Every single Broadway twinkle light shines like the star of Bethlehem.

"Well," I hear me say. "Yes. I am."

My laughter returns like the tide. I know, in this moment, confirmation of my life beyond measure. She has, with one question, washed away two decades of feelings of inadequacy. Poor as a church mouse, I have, apparently, looked wealthy to the world.

"But," I say, "let me rephrase the question. Do people say I have money?"

"Yes," she says, "they do."

"Well," I say, "I don't. And I never have."

Up Broadway, I tell her something of how I have lived these years. How I have spent my resources and then some time and again. How a priest helped me turn a corner by saying, "You must learn to receive." My fears, embarrassments. How horrible faithlessness feels.

At Twenty-third Street, we hug before going our separate ways. The stars are still close. I thank God and each one. "That's the best opening on Broadway I've ever attended," I whisper in the moonlight.

I walk home, for the first time ever, as the rich person I now know myself to be.

. . . . . .

Whole Milk
· · · · · ·

WE ARE WHO WE ARE, deep inside ourselves as well as in the mirror on the wall. We emerge throughout our lives. Sometimes, we fish for ourselves deep within ourselves. Sometimes, who we are rises to the top, like cream in whole milk. When whole milk arrives in a gallon jar on your doorstep on a Missouri morning, it's all there. Fishing for the cream won't work. The milk must be allowed to settle. In its own time, the cream rises to the top.

Who we are, like cream risen to the top, can be shocking, impossible to understand. Sometimes we recognize ourselves, see that this is who we have always been. This feels like welcoming a piece of ourselves home.

Not so long ago, I found myself walking to the window, listening intently to the skateboard practice that comes nightly to my city street. "My tea is nearly ready / and the sun has left the sky; / it's time to take the window / to see Leerie going by...." I heard myself reciting and laughed aloud.*

I went on for all that I could remember. "For every night at teatime / and before you take your seat, / with lantern and with ladder, / he comes posting up the street / ...But I, when I am stronger / and can choose what I'm to do, / O Leerie, I'll go round at night / and light the lamps with you."

Then, I edited. "O Leerie, I'll go round at night and skate the streets with you."

Suddenly, I could see me between five and nine years old, on Kansas Street in Liberty, Missouri. I loved those streets. I loved this poem, thought it mine for these streets. I would say it for sunset, dreaming of bygone days. I would edit it, add new adventures for "when I

---

* Robert Louis Stevenson, *A Child's Garden of Verses*, "The Lamplighter," The Platt and Munk Co., Inc, New York, 1929, 53.

· · · · · ·

am stronger and can choose what I'm to do." For the Jewel Tea driver, for instance, who brought salt-rising bread to the door. "O Leerie, I'll go round on streets and drive the truck with you."

When I was nine, we moved from the village to a tiny farm just outside of town. I was devastated. I lost the life I loved and I knew it: sidewalks for skating, the creek behind the house, walking to school where a miniature Statue of Liberty greeted us all. My parents and my brother were in bliss and I knew it. They did everything possible to make me happy and I knew that, too. At seventeen, I left that house without a blink for college and the city streets of Minneapolis. At twenty-nine, I wept for relief at the sight of Liberty herself, landed at home on the streets of New York City.

I have hugged these streets for a quarter of a century. Of course my laughter rises when I hear me say, "O Leerie, I'll go round at night and skate the streets with you." I realize that I have been this child with a passion for city and village streets all my life. This is who I am, risen to the top of me, like cream in whole milk.

When who I am rises in me not so attractively, and it does, sorry to say, I have options. I can let it be, accepting of myself, or try to change it. This time, the cream in whole milk is my treasure. I welcome me home and whisper, "O Leerie, I'll go round on streets and see myself with you."

· · · · · ·

LIVING IN SOCIETY and culture is just the way it is. And the way it is, in society and culture, means that we always do politics, business and theology. We don't have to like it. We don't even have to notice it. We do have to do it. We do politics, for instance, every time we schedule lunch, negotiating a date and a place and a time. Any exchange of energy—time or money or service—constitutes business. Any reference to power outside or beyond that of the culture constitutes doing theology. The millennium does not matter. The amounts of energy exchanged do not matter. Numbers do not matter here at all—how many people, how many dollars, how many times. Doing politics, business and theology goes with human territory. It has been so since we lived in caves.

I wonder when we began to put big capital letters on these words and think that Other People do them—Politics, Business and Theology. Perhaps, when our societies and cultures began to feel large. When we lived in caves, we could pretty much see everybody. Then, surely, we did not designate a cave down the way as a multinational corporation, assuming that They did Business and we didn't. Or did we? The records left on cave walls do not tell us. "The world is made less of nouns than of verbs," James Hillman has said.[*] The records left on cave walls bespeak us in verbs. Figures run, slay other creatures and eat them, light fires. There are no words at all, much less nouns with capital letters.

"Everything is everything," Sara Little, matriarch of Christian Education from the Union Theological Seminary in Richmond, Virginia once said. "Everything is everything" goes with human territory, too. Whether we like it or not, we live in an extremely coherent universe. We are one body in creation, in the cosmos. We are interrelated, interdependent, intertwined. All

---

[*] James Hillman, *The Soul's Code: In Search of Character and Calling*, Random House, New York, 1996, 86.

the residents of this universe, sentient or not, are bound by the same four forces: gravity, strong nuclear force, weak nuclear force, electromagnetism. We are all composed of the same four elements: earth, fire, air and water. We are in constant motion, woven as one fabric in interlocking patterns.

In human territory, we measure time, clock seasons, name multinational corporations for our own satisfaction. And, perhaps, for our sanity. It is hard enough to live in society as it is, knowing the month and what we do. God alone knows how it would be in this extremely coherent, ever-expanding universe were it one big undifferentiated stew. I am grateful for Genesis 1:1–2:3 and all the care God takes in differentiation: water from water, light from light, star and season and seed.

Things we call "coincidences" tell the truth about our extremely coherent universe, how "everything is everything." We hold the illusion that they are the exceptions in our lives. Actually, this is the way it is. In our universe, coincidences are the rule. The convergence of events and meaning is the cosmos knocking on our door, insisting that we notice. Coincidences strip away our illusion that everything is not everything.

Coincidences are our wake-up call. "Invest meaning in the ordinary," the cultural anthropologist Mircia Eliade is said to have said. When we do this, coincidences proliferate. We become aware of our interrelationships, our interdependencies. Everything begins to look like everything. We can even see ourselves doing it all—business, theology and politics. "They" become us. Big capital letters no longer feel necessary. We do it all. Look at that verb.

WHEN I GREW UP in beautiful downtown Liberty, Missouri, there were a handful of regulations that ruled behavior in the town. Liberty—somewhat ironically named—was dominated by the Baptists and it knew right from wrong.

No dancing, no card-playing, no pants briefer than Bermuda shorts. For the women from the college on the hill, no smoking within the city limits. No underwire brassieres. The Bible was always referenced. So it was that all the college dances were held at the high school, short shorts and smoky hazes abounded in the nearby truck stops and neighboring towns. You-know-what was not forbidden because procreation was mandated by the Bible. So, too, it was that pregnancy turned up nearly as often as the morning sun.

I chafed at the rules that filled my atmosphere. I watched friends return shorts deemed too short. I always wondered who could tell about the underwire brassieres. Were there "undercover" agents who could tell there was too much support? Nasty rubber girdles that came wrapped up in a tube and snapped like a turtle were allowed. Weren't these support, too?

These days, it falls to me to teach the Bible to all denominations. Procreation is indeed mandated by the Bible, back there in our beginnings. Dancing is back there, too. Major life decisions are even made by what we would call "throwing dice." Clothes are not a biblical issue. The length of pants is never discussed. Brassieres have yet to be a twinkle in the fashion industry's eye.

Support, however, is a biblical issue everywhere. The midwives support Moses' mother in the bulrushes. Joseph's brothers sell him off, are anything but supportive. Once sold, Joseph supports Pharaoh in a time of famine. Ruth leaves her homeland for support of Naomi, her mother-in-law. And isn't Jesus support, incarnate? Tax collectors, women, the lame, the blind, the ill, the possessed—Jesus is there to support everyone. Except, if you please, the rule-makers.

· · · · ·

Brandishing the Bible for the making of rules is one of the points here. This is always a little dangerous. The Bible is large, full of all sorts of behavior. The minute we make a rule from one part of the Bible, someone somewhere else is breaking it. How would it be if we made rules only from King David's behavior? Ooh, dangerous.

The other point here, playing on the word, is that the people of God are called to support, not make rules against it. To be Christ's own body, we are called to support each other in all ways imaginable. Then, what is truly supportive is tricky business. Too much care can look supportive and render a child arrested as an adult. Too little care can look irresponsible and prove the making of the child in later years. Al-Anon has taught us all to be careful about our interdependencies.

For our call to seek and to offer support, the Bible is helpful, far more useful than for the making of rules. If we let the making and keeping of rules go, the Bible can be our family album for life and for love. All those years ago and dominated by one behavior-conscious denomination, I did not know this. I knew only the rules, the judgment. So it was that I scurried to the nearest Episcopal Church in a nearby town on the first day I could drive. Never mind for support, this was for survival.

For all these years, I have kept Richard Hooker's words under my pillow: "By the goodness of Almighty God and His servant Elizabeth, we are."[*] The shape and structure of my underwear is my business. Support is Christian business.

---

[*] Dedication to Book V, *The Laws of Ecclesiastical Polity*, 1597.

WHEN THE YEARS at General Seminary were complete, I left with the family album under my arm. I moved into a congregation to do Christian education, knowing I hadn't a clue. All I had was my Bible and my faith that it was our family album for life and love. I hoped to slide into this foreign territory quietly.

Not to be. "You're in charge of the Christmas pageant," the rector said as he was ready to leave on vacation.

I was horrified. "I do Greek and Hebrew, I don't do Christmas pageants."

He smiled. "You do Christmas pageants now," he said.

So I did. I called the Sunday School teachers together, made brownies and coffee. Within minutes, I knew this was all I had to do. These women did the Christmas pageant and knew it all: where the costumes were, who was good at speaking parts, whose turn it was to be the Virgin Mary.

Content to be the convener, I offered the little I could contribute. I opened the family album, talked about how it takes a blend of two gospels to make a pageant. "Matthew and Luke have very different things to say about Jesus' birth," I said.

These women knew the family album about as well as I knew the pageant. We read the stories aloud together. Then we got excited about how Sunday School could inform the pageant. We designed ways to teach the birth stories Sunday by Sunday through Pentecost. We wanted these kids to know the stories before they walked them down the aisle.

It was Advent when I got word that the Virgin Mary had refused to play her role. "You'd better come over," her mother said on my answering machine.

"Why ever don't you want to be the Virgin Mary?" I asked. She was still in her school uniform, just home from fourth grade.

· · · · · ·

"I've been thinking about it," she said. "I don't want to be the only mother whose baby lives. All those other babies die. This is a terrible part to play."

I was speechless. The Sunday School curriculum was in my face. We had studied all of the first two chapters of Matthew and Luke and she had heard every word. It had never occurred to me to think of the story like this.

I took a deep breath. "Let's all go see the boss," I said. The three of us walked around the corner, sat in the rector's office.

He was amazed. "Why ever don't you want to be the Virgin Mary?" he asked.

"What are you teaching those children?" he jumped up and shouted at me the minute the words were out of her mouth.

Instantly, she stood up to face him. "It's in the Bible," she said. "It's the story."

We all sat down, looked at each other in silence.

"So," said the rector, "what are we going to do?"

"You can't leave it out," she said. "It's in the story."

"Oh, good," he said, "we'll have the only Christmas pageant in New York City with a Slaughter of the Innocents."

The fourth grader folded her hands in her lap, looked at him patiently. "You don't have to act it out," she said. "You just have to read it. People need to know it's in the story. I'll do it if we read it. I even asked my big sister. She'll read it."

So she did. That year, the real live Baby Jesus was huge and squirmy, filled every inch of the Virgin Mary's lap. While her sister read all of Matthew from the family album, the Virgin Mary drenched the baby with her tears. I counted my own tears as Christmas pageant baptism, everyone else's as gift of the Word.

. . . . . .

I AM GULLIBLE. I will believe what you tell me unless I have a good reason not to. I learned this with "tomato soup lies." I was a junior at the University of Minnesota on a, no surprise, cold day. In the dorm lunch line with my friends, Gay and Carolyn, I all but whined, "I hope it's a good lunch."

"Oh, it is," Gay said, turning to face me. "It's the best—tomato soup and grilled cheese, cinnamon rolls for dessert."

Oh, yes, the best. Sanford Hall had some awful white meals for lunch. This one had color and taste and oh, yum, homemade dessert. We chatted, waited our turn.

Oh, no—white meal when we arrived at last. "Gay! How could you?!" I shrieked.

"Hah, hah, hah, you believed me!" she crowed.

"I had no choice," I wailed. "I had no reason not to believe you." Hours later, I was still outraged. "Furthermore," I said to her infuriating grin, "I'll never believe you again." Did I? I do remember testing everything she said, asking "Is this a tomato soup lie?"

I became skeptical. Then, I hated being skeptical. I hated not trusting, the way skeptical felt—suspicious, like something was lurking around corners about to jump at me. I wanted gullible back. I wanted to trust. One day, I decided that I had to choose. If I chose to be gullible, I would be vulnerable to tomato soup lies, lies out of the blue.

So I have. Decades and decades later, I still choose gullible, with vulnerability as its price. I will believe what you tell me unless I have a good reason not to. When I am fooled by a lie out of the blue, I chalk it up. It goes with gullible territory. I work at being trusting; it feels better.

Did Gay's tomato soup lie set me thinking about truth and lies forever? Maybe so. Certainly, all these years later, Pilate's question of Jesus is mine as well: "What is truth?" (John 18:38)

. . . . . .

Jesus is close to crucifixion when he is asked. Long before, at table with his friends, he has given the answer: "I am the way, the truth, and the life..." (John 14:6) Jesus as the truth is clear. Tomato soup lies are clear, too. Sometimes, not much else is. Pilate never gets an answer. I wonder about truth and lies to this day.

"That which is really true is seldom obvious," I am quoted as saying. I no longer recall the context in which these words arrived. But I do know that the universe is extremely complex and coherent, that a lot is going on all the time. Some of what is going on all the time is obvious, but not all the truth. I have learned to look at what is going on and ask where the deep truth might be.

I also know that many truths can exist simultaneously, even appear to be contradictory. Sitting on a multicultural faculty table has taught me to look for more than one truth in every conversation. At least.

I have learned that truth can shatter. What is called a lie can heal and make whole. Like mercury from a broken thermometer, the difference between truth and lie can be slippery. I have seen lies that turn out to be truth waiting to be born.

"What is truth?" is a good question, always worth asking. Like Pilate, we may end up without an answer. In the meantime, Jesus gets to be truth. I get to be gullible.

Living, Really

· · · · · ·

AT NEW YORK THEOLOGICAL SEMINARY, the curriculum is designed to give God a turn. Most of our classes are at night, we rent our space, the tuition is low. If you have a B.A. and can bear a multicultural, ardently Christian milieu, we will let you come and try. This is called pretty-much-open admissions.

And everybody comes, more bodies than our classrooms can hold. The old, the young, Spanish speakers, Korean speakers. Male and female, both flavors of God's one image, whether they can stand each other or not. Sometimes thirteen Baptist denominations appear at the drop of a hat. God, being no fool, takes every turn possible. In my experience, there are always blessings and surprises. When God takes a turn, I often find me changing my mind.

Years ago, I was pressured to make an appointment for an admissions interview. I resisted. "We have pretty-much-open admissions," I said. "She doesn't need an interview with me."

"She's on crutches," I was told.

This was not enough to make me change my mind. "No matter," I replied. "My colleague in the biblical field who survived childhood polio is on crutches, too."

"She needs to see you," I was told.

"No, not really," I insisted. "I'll drop off the forms. Tell her to send them in."

The sweet voice of the New York Theological Seminary landlord insisted. We rent, after all, so I relented. I changed my mind.

She came, on crutches. We talked about the school, the schedule, the bizarre and wondrous student body. About how we work out multicultural life together, how we pray. How the curriculum is designed so God can take a turn. "So," I said, "here are the forms. Fill them out and send them in." I sat back and smiled.

· · · · · ·

There was a little silence. "Do you really think they will accept me?" she asked.

"Really," I said.

"But I'm dying," she said.

The silence became mine. "Well," I heard me say, "we are all dying."

"But I am really dying," she said.

"Well," I heard me say, suspecting that this was one of God's turns, "we are all really dying. We call this living, but we are all really dying. Perhaps you are to come here to help us remember."

Years and more kinds of ministry later, she spoke to me of her love of biblical translation and teaching. "If I had a future," she said, "I would do this."

Right out of my mouth came God's turn, again. "None of us has a future," I heard me say. "You do this now. All each of us has is a now."

I live differently in the now since she came to seminary. More often than before, I remember that we are really dying. I treasure the truth of autumn, the chance to watch really living while dying right up front. The seasons are God's turn, too, I've come to think. Like minds, they need to change.

Turning, the changing of seasons and the changing of minds—these define the biblical word we know as "repentance." "Even when you saw it," Jesus challenges in the temple, "you did not then change your mind and believe..." (Matthew 21:32) When God takes a turn, I want to see it and believe. I want to be able to turn, to repent, change my mind. These days, when the future creeps into my mind or my words, I check in on the now. I watch to see if God might be taking a turn. I look around to see if it's time to change my mind. I believe this is living, really.

. . . . .

I NEEDED HELP. "Dissertation?" I wailed at God. "What is a dissertation?" I went on about all the things I had done, left undone, how "scholarly" was not a word anyone had ever used about me. "You do the choreography," I implored, "I need help."

Whatever did I expect as answer to these prayers? "Scholarly" advice, I guess. But God's ways are not our ways. Help arrived on a motorcycle. I took it, was thankful for it. Here was a brand new friend, swagger in his steps. "I'm here for Minka," he would all but growl to the front desk of the General Theological Seminary. The very idea made me thrill. Such choreography, such a God.

I lightened up, laughed easily, took my days step by step. This was help, indeed. Some days, I even forgot I didn't know how to do what I was doing. And then, the friendship was fabulous.

It was ironic, this friendship, and I knew it. This man couldn't believe that I went to what he insisted on calling "God School."

"I didn't even know there were God Schools," he said once, shaking his head.

I laughed. "Neither did I until I fell into one," I said.

From time to time, "all your degrees" crept into his words. This sounded to me a little like condemnation. I would think of the "first degree" in a trial. "So?" I would say, a little defensively.

"I don't have any," he always said.

"You have other things, other gifts," I always said in return, knew this to be true.

It was a great intense friendship, but not a very long one. We went our separate ways with love and laughter. "All your degrees" landed in our good-byes. I knew then, as I had all along the way, how ironic this was. "Formal" education was not on this man's résumé, not yet, anyway, among his gifts. Neither was "religion." My combination of the two made him nervous and he said so.

On the other hand, I learned a lot from this man and I said so, every time it happened. He was wise and deeply spiritual. Once, when I was confessing my fears about a huge liturgy for which I had some responsibility, he changed my understanding of faithfulness forever.

We were at lunch. I got all my anxiety out on the table between us. He stopped the cheeseburger midway between plate and mouth and looked at me like I had landed from Mars. I could read his thoughts as they traveled across his forehead. He was clearly thinking something like, "Who is this woman? All those degrees and in God School and she doesn't know this?!"

He put the cheeseburger down. Grinning, he patted my hand like I was seven years old. "Fear," he said, "is lack of faith." My help to this very day.

And then, he taught me to pray.

My feelings of inadequacy immobilizing me on another occasion, he growled, "Say this prayer, sweetheart, every night before you sleep: Thank you, dear God, for this day. I did the best I knew how to do. I know that you know it. If this is all there is, it is enough."

Even when my best hardly feels good enough, I can say these words and sleep. To this day. Almost every day, I have trouble with the last line, I still want more.

I confess: I wanted more of this friendship, too. Hard as it was to let it go, however, I wouldn't have missed it for the world. For me, it was the answer to prayer. For him? I think the little dissertation that sits on the GTS Library shelf is his first degree.

· · · · · ·

"WHAT'S WRONG, MINKA?" Andrew was following me out of the sacristy, across the choir room.

"Nothing," I said. We had done weekday Morning Prayer. It was my turn to officiate.

"I know better," he said. "Something's wrong. I'll make coffee."

"I'll take coffee," I said, opening the door to the stairwell to the church house apartments where each of us lived. "But nothing is wrong."

I dropped off my cassock and prayer book at home. When I knocked on his door, I could smell the coffee. Yum.

He poured. "Give it up," he said. "I watched you at Morning Prayer."

I laughed. "Can you read my mind while you watch me officiate at Morning Prayer?"

Laughing in return, he pushed my coffee across the table. "Yes. Yes, I can."

I was really tickled. Maybe he could teach me this. "How, Andrew? Just how do you read the mind of the officiant at Morning Prayer?"

He set down his cup. "Here's how," he replied. "I was watching you across the choir. You looked like you were enjoying yourself, all the way into the Lord's Prayer. When you said, 'thy kingdom come, thy will be done,' your face totally changed. It looked like this."

Andrew wrinkled his face like a raisin, scrunched up every muscle. He cowered. He looked like Mount Everest was about to land on him. I screamed with laughter.

"The minute you were into 'on earth as in heaven,'" he said, "you relaxed. Something, Minka, is wrong. What is it?"

"Okay," I said. "You read my face, not my mind. And 'wrong' is too strong a word here."

"Okay," Andrew said, "I read your face. 'Wrong' may be too strong a word, but something is going on. What is it?"

· · · · · ·

"Oh, Andrew," I said. "You know the expression, 'be careful what you pray for, you may get it'? It's true."

I told him how really careful I had been about this prayer. How long, how deep I went before I specifically prayed for love. How gingerly I talked to God. How, in a flash, my prayer had been answered. How little I now realized I had known before the prayer had been uttered. How very full my plate was, how complicated my life was as a result.

"I'm totally out of my league," I bemoaned. "No wonder you can read my face on 'thy kingdom come, thy will be done.' I'll never ever take these words lightly again."

The expression, "be careful what you pray for," honors the depth and complexity of God's universe. As observant, careful and loving as we may be, more than we know is always going on in our lives. "Thy kingdom come, thy will be done" is an open invitation for God to stir up the pot.

This is the God, I remind myself, who says, "Do not remember the former things or consider the things of old. I am about to do a new thing; now it springs forth, do you perceive it?" (Isaiah 43:18–19)

I want to perceive it. I certainly do not want to pray for anything not of God's kingdom, God's will. I have, on the rarest of rare occasions, prayed specifically. When I have been so desperate or courageous, I have surrounded the request with "thy kingdom come, thy will be dones." For these prayers, I have never ever moved out of the conditional mood: "should" this be in my best interest, "might" this be in your divine-design, dear God.

I never have taken these open invitation words lightly again. Read my face.

. . . . . .

"YOU LIKE ISLANDS, Mom," my son said to me one day. "What does that mean?"

I hadn't thought about it, but he is right. I live on one, scurry to others when I can. Long Beach, Key West and Manhattan Islands all hold my heart. "Huh," I heard me say, "maybe I just feel best on the edge?"

And what might that mean?

The grandfather in Margaret Coleus's story of the Arapaho talks of this: "We are edge people. We live at the edge of two worlds, white and Arapaho. It is hard to remember who we are when we dwell in the edge space."[*] Living between cultures and peoples means never living in the middle of either. It is belonging, but not fitting in.

I grew up smack in the middle of the United States, right between the Missouri and the Mississippi Rivers. Like the Arapaho, I grew up between disparate cultures. My mother's people were old Missourians, originally Virginia colonists, who made their way west. By the time I came along, there had been eight or nine of these generations, even a legitimate claim for land in the Cherokee Nation. My father's people were American newcomers. His parents worked on land belonging to Czar Nicholas II of Russia. On this side of my family, I count as a second generation American. The foods, religions, and family customs of these cultures were different. Christmas and Easter, even, were on different dates each year.

As a child, it was not remembering who I was that was my problem. It was the abundance and the variety that got in my way. Over the years, I tried it all out. Sometimes I was northerner, sometimes southerner. Sometimes Russian, sometimes Indian. Sometimes immigrant, sometimes native. Sometimes reformed, sometimes catholic. I am who I am because of the

---

[*] Margaret Coleus, *The Ghost Walker*, Berkley Books, New York, 1996, 106.

abundance and variety in my upbringing. Rarely, however, have I been able to stand in the middle of any of it for long. Unless I can get to the edge, it feels as if there isn't enough of the truth.

No wonder I am a fervent Episcopalian. All the churches of the Anglican Communion hold both the reformed and catholic Christian traditions. Anglicans everywhere can echo the Arapaho grandfather's words. With both reformed and catholic ways, we "live at the edge of two worlds."

The edge is essential to the roles I dance in my life, too. Mother, teacher, deacon, writer— these are all vocations that ask for leadership from the edge. There are moments in each of them that come from a central or middle space. Eventually, however, I am called to the edge so that the child, the learner, the liturgy, the Word can step out on its own.

Islands—living stones in living water—are literally the edge of creation. Perhaps I seek this edge of creation to echo the way I live in my faith, in my work, in my soul?

I could do worse. There are more dangerous edges in the world, literally. I think of Fleda, the woman who leaves her house and all its furnishings to live in a tent pitched next to the whirlpool of Niagara Falls.[*] Islands look a lot safer to me than this.

Maybe, islands fit in the list of the wondrous groups to which I belong—gay men, children, subways, musicians. If so, they get the prize as the farthest out. Literally.

---

[*] Jane Urquhart, *The Whirlpool*, McClelland and Stuart Inc., Toronto, 1997.

· · · · · ·

I FOUND THE WORDS for the difference between "belonging" and "fitting" in a room packed with gay men of faith, the banquet dinner in celebration of Integrity International. There were famous people in the room. Not me. I was not famous, not gay, not male. I did not fit. I was simply the banquet speaker.

I basically said this when it came time for my words. "The only thing that qualifies me for this honor," I said, "is that in many ways I am my father's oldest son. But there is no way you could know that. How did I get here? Why are you my group?"

There was wonderful laughter. I told them how I qualified as the oldest son, how the first-born of a professional athlete is bound to be reared in locker rooms. I told them how the gay world and its issues were among the ironies I met when I came to New York City in 1974. How life in this diverse city helped me learn, to my horror, exclusion everywhere. I had known racism on arrival. I was, however, shockingly naive about women's place in history. I told them how, much to my surprise, I discovered joy and freedom in the Bible. With them, too. I told them how I despaired as a child, sure of never fitting in. I told them how much I had learned from gay men, how grateful I was.

"This is the point," I said, "you are my group. I do not fit in with you as a group, but I belong to you and you to me. This is why God is born in Bethlehem. This is why Jesus walks, why he dies. There is no 'except this one or that one' on the cross. We are one. Whether we fit in with each other or not, we belong to each other. Your invitation to me demonstrates that the glory of this saving life and death is true."

I walked home a little stunned by it all. The gift of the invitation, the shared laughter, the learning through my own words. I had seen me "do theology" here, put my life and their lives right up front and talk about who God is and how and why. I saw me confidently distinguish between fitting in and belonging. I saw me walk home alone, sure sign of not fitting in. It was okay.

I began to watch. Where else might I belong? Did I fit in or not? Lots of places, it turned out. What might I learn about myself in these places of belonging that surprises me? A lot here, too.

Not so long after, please, I turned up with a room in a monastery, learning Benedictine spirituality and how to cook for forty people at a time. I went from seminary to belong with children, their freedom and their truth. I now know that I belong on subways with people who do not speak my language. I belong teaching in a mix of Christian traditions. In public, I appear to belong with musicians and they can all tell you that I can barely sing. I could go on and on.

One of the differences between belonging and fitting in is length of time. I don't get to be with any of these groups of people forever, even though I belong. In rooms of gay men or nine-year-olds in Sunday School and certainly in monasteries, the time comes when I leave, I move on. I get no illusion of eternity, "until death do us part." Or, maybe, death does us part? Death seems a very big word for the end of a time together; "parting is such sweet sorrow" feels like a gentler way to say this.

The sweet of this sorrow is the truth of resurrection. We can say that death has lost its sting because we know that resurrection is around the corner. In this life as well as in the life to come. There are new and wondrous groups around every corner for resurrection. This is God's enormous world, God's divine-design. There is more time and so much more space. How fitting for this great, big God.

. . . . . .

IN 1987, I spent most of Epiphany—the season of light—in Belfast, Ireland. This was bright light; a lot, for me, came into it.

The Anglican Communion, to begin with. I cherish the Anglican Communion, the twenty-seven churches from around the world who gather by way of bishops, from time to time, at Lambeth Palace in England. I even teach the Communion—King Henry's calling us out, the leadership of Elizabeth I giving us the liturgy that binds us as a Communion across time and space. I loved it, but I had never seen it.

Young people from these twenty-seven Anglican churches gathered prior to the 1988 Lambeth meeting of bishops. Belfast was chosen as the site to show a commitment to the troubled truth of our times. Adult facilitators were garnered; I got to be one. In January 1987, we would talk and worship our brains out. Anglican youth would, as a result, present themselves by paper and in delegation a year later.

The event began with worship. There were hundreds of people in the room, politics and races and languages from around the world. "The Lord be with you," the Archbishop of All Ireland said.

"And with thy spirit," we replied in one voice. I burst into tears. The Anglican Communion had just burst into the light. We really were one body, bound by the words of the Book of Common Prayer. It felt like a miracle. It was an epiphany.

Belfast was an epiphany, too. Rage behind eyes, tanks on the streets, the possibility of explosion every moment, every day. Such a hard life.

Then, I learned myself anew as an American woman in Belfast. By day, we met and deliberated. By night, I went to pubs with women. All of this, please, in a clergy collar. "Please do this," the Archbishop had said to me. "People may never get another chance to see it."

· · · · · ·

At the pub, we would tuck into a corner, a group would gather. Eventually, I noticed that I was hearing the same stories from women night after night, awful stories of abusive relationships. Their lives were hard, just like Belfast's streets.

After more than a week of hearing these stories night after night, I cracked. More of the same—grisly detail after detail. We talked about support groups, books, spiritual advisors. Finally, I saw me cover this woman's hand with my own. "Leave," I said.

They acted like Martians had landed in the room. Shock was on every face. I had said the unthinkable.

I was shocked in return. "People leave all the time," I said. I talked about co-dependency, the hard truth I had learned from Al-Anon in the United States. How sometimes, healing can only happen when we refuse to be part of other people's abusive paths. "Sometimes," I insisted, "we must leave."

No one would hear of it.

Suddenly, I realized that I was not in the Americas. I was in the place from which Americans had come. All I could think of was how all my people, over three centuries and for whatever reasons, had left. I was in a room full of people whose people had stayed. The word "pioneer" took on new meaning for me that night. So, too, the phrase, "land of the brave and the free."

I all but hung out the airplane window in Epiphany light as we flew home. I needed to see Ellis Island, the Statue of Liberty. To this day, I harbor the fantasy that Liberty wore her collar, smiled and waved back.

. . . . . .

IT TAKES BRAVE to be free. "By the means of freedom Christ has freed you," Paul says to the Galatians, "Stand, therefore, and do not again become entangled by a yoke of slavery." (5:1) Ooh, easier said than done.

Living in society of any sort, as we must, is the problem. Setting ourselves free from bondage is a lifetime endeavor. We can be entangled in slavery to our work, our roles, our personal habits. "Watch it," he admonishes.

"There is neither Jew nor Greek, there is neither slave nor free, there is neither male and female," he has triumphantly claimed earlier in the letter, "all, therefore, all of you are one by the means of Christ Jesus." (3:28) This is a shocking claim for people in the Roman Empire in the middle of the first century. Greeks are privileged; Jews are not. Men head households; women are counted as their property. The population of the Empire at the time is estimated at fifty-four million; one third of these people are slaves. How does Christ Jesus change this? What can Paul possibly mean?

I suspect that the Apostle asked himself these very questions. I am sure that he means it. But I'll bet you he himself had to think these astonishing words all the way through after he said them. His first letter to the Corinthians follows the letter to Galatia. A tiny phrase buried in 7:29–31 suggests the Apostle has thought about it. "As-if-not" is the way the Greek reads, a little hard to see in the English translation:

> From now on, let even those who have wives be as though they had none, and those who mourn as though they were not mourning, and those who rejoice as though they were not rejoicing, and those who buy as though they had no possessions, and those who deal with the world as though they had no dealings with it.

· · · · · ·

"As though none" barely makes Paul's point. He is not advocating withdrawal from society. The Corinthians must live in society, as must we all. "As-if-not" is how to remember that our culture is never all there is, never sets the bottom lines of human reality. Beyond marriage, business, the throes of tumultuous feelings of grief and joy is God's universe. This is why he ends the verse with the words, "the form of this world is passing away."

I take this to mean that Christ Jesus changes what we know about life. It's real and true, we're in it. It is not, however, all the life there is. Even more, the roles and work and events of this life do not get to tell us who we are. Christ Jesus gets the last word here. We are—no matter the role, the religion, the economic status and certainly not the gender—one body.

We are to live our lives as if who we are and what we do is not all that is true. We are to watch it, to see that we do not become entangled in who we are and what we do to the point of bondage. We are to stand for the freedom for which Jesus died—human lives that are more life and more potential than we can ask or imagine. We are called to be brave and free.

So, how? Memory of as-if-not is our hope. Once we remember that we are free, we can hold onto hope. Then, whatever gets us through the night. Anything we can do to make space in our lives to inhale deeply, breathe freely, and stretch our minds as far as they will go.

This takes bravery. It is hard to let love of any kind go. Saying "no"—to those we love or respect or for whom we work—is awful. Changing roles means we must choose to be vulnerable, if not regularly foolish. Commitment bears risk.

"It takes brave to be free" echoes the United States' national anthem. There is a second verse we never sing that I found on the very last page of my hymnal. These last words to sing in the book will do here, too: "this be our motto, 'In God is our trust.'"*

---

* *The Hymnal 1982*, official hymnal of the Episcopal Church, #720.

I ACTUALLY FOUND MYSELF SINGING "I've grown accustomed to his face" one day, walking down the street. I was thinking about a man I had met and it made me laugh out loud. These are words that Rex Harrison sings in the musical *My Fair Lady*, words that I have edited to suit my situation. In both Rex Harrison's situation and my own, a translation of these words might be, "I'm hooked."

This is a different kind of emotional reality than the one that passes when seventy-two hours have elapsed. This is the kind of physical attraction that warrants the phrase, "animal magnetism." Waiting for seventy-two hours to pass does no good at all.

The magnetism of "animal magnetism" is a very real phenomenon. Magnets attract each other and "hook" to each other. When I am strongly attracted to someone, the energy feels electromagnetic to me. Circumstances determine whether this is good or bad. The potential for enduring unions lies in this force. So does the potential for addiction, the need for more. The potential for obsession lurks here as well, the need to possess at all costs. Rarely are obsessions "magnificent" as in the classic movie with Rock Hudson and Jane Wyman. Whether we are the pursuer or the pursued in obsession, it is apt to be awful. We have problems when the hooked, however and whatever it is, is not magnificent.

Driven by this energy of attraction, it feels like I am on my own in the universe. The opposite, actually, is true: for some reason that I may or may not ever understand, I am hooked to someone else. To become unhooked, all I know to do is to pray, ask that I may learn what I am to learn. Then, over and over and over again, I say the words given to me by my musician friend, Mary Jane: "Say 'thank you,' Minka, and let go."

I think of this as physics of the soul. "Mom's physics," my mathematical son once charitably said with a smile. Four kinds of energy bind creation and the cosmos, hold it togeth-

. . . . . .

er, keep it moving. Hardly a scientist, I work to understand this. Gravity is friendliest for me, the attraction of all matter for all matter over time and space. Because it is far-reaching, it is the dominant force. At the same time, it is the weakest of these forces. My amateur's view is that the way gravity looks strong and really is weak offers one explanation for how Jesus can walk on water.

Strong nuclear force and weak nuclear force continue to baffle me. One of these two forces, forgive me, has to do with the way Crazy Glue works.

Hooked by attraction, my soul knows how the fourth force feels. Faraday and Maxwell unified electricity and magnetism into the single theory of electromagnetism in the nineteenth century, proved that electromagnetic forces both attract and repel. Sometimes, hooked feels electric to me and my body tingles. Other times, I recognize the magnetic, drawn to another person the way iron filings race toward a magnet. The reassuring physics here is that over long distances, electromagnetic forces cancel each other out. Eventually, "Say 'thank you,' and let go" works.

As a Christian, I claim that love is the binding energy of the universe. The force of love is why God created, why Jesus was willing to die, why God's own breath is poured out into us all. I feel this energy by way of all the forces that bind us—humans, creation, the very stars. In gravity, over space and time. Hooked, electromagnetically, even. Knowing that love is a unified field of force in the universe is one thing, explaining it is another thing entirely. I stand here on my faith and expect it to work. I use Crazy Glue the same way, by faith.

. . . . . .

ONE EASTERTIDE, Sister Mary Michael wrote and asked me about forgiveness. "I'm right, am I not," she said, "that Jesus commands the Father to forgive from the cross in Luke 23:34?" I had not thought about this before. I looked up the verse in the Greek and she was absolutely right: Jesus speaks from the cross in the imperative mood. This is a direct command: "Father, forgive them for they know not what they do."

Her Good Friday sermon had been challenged. She knew I was graduating from seminary after thousands of words about Luke-Acts, so she wrote. She needed to talk this out, having been challenged for suggesting that Jesus is doing the hard work of dying. Perhaps, she said, Jesus commands the Father to forgive until he is able to do it for himself. Perhaps, she had proclaimed, we all understand this: knowing that asking forgiveness is appropriate, asking God to do it for us until we can do it for ourselves.

I had never thought about this before, either. I had heard a million other Good Friday words about these Words from the Cross. "Look how wonderful Jesus is," these words essentially all said. "Even in agony, he is taking care of others." No one had ever talked about the command, the verb in the imperative mood. No one ever suggested that Jesus was telling God to do this because he was busy suffering, busy dying.

I did, as Sister Mary Michael suggested, understand this. In the very moment her letter arrived, there were events in my life I could not yet forgive. Her words gave me a way to hand it all over to God. Good enough for Jesus, it was good enough for me. With her letter in my hand, I did it: "Dear God, please forgive them, I know they didn't mean to hurt me. I promise to work on this forgiveness myself."

Thanks to Sister Mary Michael, I began to watch forgiveness carefully—where it was, what it was, how it was offered. Thanks to Dolores, I have now even sung it.

. . . . .

The word had come up over and over again in the second semester Greek class. There was Jesus from the cross, commanding the Father to forgive. There was the vinedresser in the parable commanding the owner, "Sir, forgive it for one more year until I dig around it and put manure on it." (Luke 13:8) In controversy over the anointing of Jesus feet, there was the command to Judas, "Forgive her..." (John 12:7)

We discovered that the one Greek verb here and elsewhere could have all these meanings: to forgive, to leave alone, to let be, to let loose/give vent, to divorce, to legally remit, to dissolve, to disband, to shed. We learned that Jesus often commands forgiveness and we do not see it in our English translations. We see phrases like "leave it alone" or "let her be." We were amazed. When we heard "let her be," Dolores exclaimed aloud from the back of the room. "Let her be! Let it be!" she exuberantly said. "It's the Beatles!"

For the final class celebration, Dolores arrived with a gigantic boom box and a drum. She handed around sheet music in Greek: "When I find myself in times of trouble, Mother Mary comes to me, speaking words of wisdom, let it be, let it be..." Dolores drummed away with her instrumentation booming behind us, we sang the Beatles in Greek: "Forgive, forgive, there will be an answer, let it be, let it be."

Leaving something alone or letting it be is a far cry from saying, "It's okay. Never mind." Forgiveness as we have it in the New Testament offers us time and space to heal. Jesus offers us a way to hand over this work to God.

I could sing this, too: "Sister Mary Michael comforts me..."

· · · · · ·

PEOPLE WHO FORAGE on my city streets break my heart. I cannot bear the idea of living this way. Then, there is something scary about witnessing such lives, a reminder that we are animals. We are the only creatures in Genesis 1:1–2:3 that are not named by the way we move. After creepers, swimmers, flyers and walkers, we are named "image" and "likeness" of God. We are, nonetheless, animals. Animals foraging for food or clothes or a warm spot in which to sleep look desperate. Deep inside myself I recognize the desperate, become afraid.

Years ago, Gary Zukav taught me to work hard not to judge foragers, insisting that we can never know why another person makes such life choices.[*] My responsibility is to work so that these people have other options in my society. It is not my responsibility to make them live a certain way. Once I remember this, I can put my broken heart back in place. Then, I become grateful that they remind me that I am making choices about my life all the time. I want to be grateful for my blessings. I want to remember that I, too, am an animal.

Around the same time as the Zukav learning, the Dean of the Cathedral of St. John the Divine preached one of the more useful sermons I have ever heard. I recall him making many of the same points that Zukav makes: resist judgment and work for fundamental change in society. And then, glory, he offered a strategy for giving on the street. There were hundreds of us in church that morning and we all got it. Coffee hour was sprinkled with conversations among strangers, all of us agreed that it was wonderful to have a plan.

The dean was clear about decision and choice, about starting each day knowing what we were willing to give away freely. "Put this in your pocket," he instructed. "When it is gone, say so. Start the next day the same way."

---

[*] Gary Zukav, *The Seat of the Soul*, Simon & Schuster, Inc., New York, 1989.

This giving strategy has served me well. When I forget to set aside what I am willing to give freely, I notice. There have been days when I have all but forced money on strangers because no one had asked. I am much less susceptible to guilt.

Having made choices about how to give makes me more aware of street life. Regularly, I mentally move me behind a shopping cart and put me out there. This is nearly as hard for me as is watching someone eat discarded food. I give up the computer, the E-mail that holds my baby sister close. I mentally give away the odd furniture I really do want my kids to cherish. I donate all these books to the Salvation Army. I anguish when I realize that no one really needs red cowboy boots when they live on the street. I hug old friends and pray our love continues. I kiss the beach and baseball games on the TV good-bye.

My secret fantasy is that physical fitness comes with life on the street, but I doubt that this is true. The best thing about my imagined homelessness is that for awhile, I do not take the details of my day-to-day life for granted. For awhile, I exult in homecoming to welcoming warmth on a winter day. I cherish the hockey jersey I forgot I owned, the luxury of undisturbed piles, sitting on the couch with my feet up.

Eventually, I forget. I take my luxurious life for granted until someone who is hungry reminds me. My heart breaks. I struggle to resist judgment, work for fundamental change. I fill my pockets with what I am willing to freely give. I thank the angels that I may.

. . . . . .

I BEGAN WORK at the Cathedral of St. John the Divine in July 1988. The first evening, the dean's grandson arrived at my front door. A dusty, smiling man stood behind him when I answered the bell. The child held architectural renderings that towered above him, fluttered in the evening breeze. "Grandpa would like for you to put these under your pillow," he said.

"Okay," I said, smiling in return. "Would you like to come in?"

"We would," said the man in a British accent. "We can explain."

The child was attentive as the man, Simon Verity, the Master Stone Carver of the Cathedral, introduced himself to me. We rolled out the renderings on top of the kitchen table. Simon showed me the twelve columns on the face of the cathedral, explaining that these 1926 drawings included carving plans for the columns. These were to be "the last of the prophets," Melchizedek to John the Baptist. "It's time to do it," Simon said. "The dean would like to think about it. He might even have said, 'meditate on it.'"

"He did," said the child.

"Would it be okay if I put them next to the bed instead of under my pillow?" I asked. "This way I won't squash them."

"I think it would," said the child.

Serious conversations ensued. We wanted to honor the original design, its intention and its time. We also wanted to update the design to reflect our time. More than half a century had passed since Cram and Ferguson had rendered these plans. In the original envisioning of these "last of the prophets," not a woman had been named. We sat on the cathedral steps in the sun and talked about getting Sarah and Hagar up there with

· · · · · ·

Abraham, setting Elijah and Elisha arm-in-arm, standing the Baptist's mother next to John.

Eventually, the carving began. One day, I returned home from teaching to a message from Simon on my answering machine: "I need for you to come and see this. Someone rather awful is twisting his way out of the stone."

I left him word that I was on my way, went for the train. On the steps, I laughed. "It's Jacob," I said, "every inch."

Simon's eyes were wide. "How did you know?"

"Oh, Simon," I said. "The craft and cunning of Jacob is all there. The twist tells his story true."

"What story?" Simon asked.

I sat down. I was already stunned by the way carving works—how the artist takes away stone and the statue emerges. Carvers cannot correct their work, patching the way sculptors can. That Jacob in all his integrity had emerged under Simon's gifted hand was pretty wonderful. How he had twisted his attractive, conniving way out of the stone without Simon's knowing the Genesis stories was beyond me.

Simon and a host of others have completed the columns. Melchizedek and John the Baptist, just like the original plans, face West 112th Street. Elizabeth stands next to John, Elijah and Elisha are arm-in-arm.

I've had those old renderings framed, they hang on my wall. I look at them to remember that our lives emerge from within us. When we named the stone column Jacob, he emerged under Simon's hand, chip by chip. His story and his soul stand there today for all the world to see. Our souls and our stories are deep inside us, too. Time and the events of our lives fashion us the way Simon sculpts away stone, chip by chip. We emerge as ourselves and stand for all the world to see.

· · · · · ·

God, for me, has been Supreme Choreographer for a long time. Since coming to the cathedral, God has also become Supreme Architect, Supreme Stone Carver, too. The way Simon sculpts stone, God fashions us. Does the divine bear the dust of stone the way carvers do? This I do not know. I know this: when I do not feel dusty, it's a good day.

Simply

· · · · · ·

VICTOR MARCHED ME OUT of the Balcony Restaurant, up Broadway. At West 112th Street, he turned me around the corner. "This is your grandfather's watch," he said, pointing to the face of the Cathedral of St. John the Divine. "Keep it running." There were no more words until we were at the top of the steps.

More than anyone but God, Victor taught me to love the church. In the decade we were friends, we shared it all. We celebrated the church; we yelled and screamed about how awful it was. In each other's arms, we cried when she broke our hearts.

We were both in theological doctoral programs. When the instructions about the cathedral as my grandfather's watch came down, he had been a priest for more than ten years. I was still refusing to consider ordination, insistent that I had all the power and authority I needed by way of my baptism. Of this, by the way, I remain certain. The difference between then and now, if one is charitable with definitions, is that I have experienced a call to the diaconate.

Victor was clear that he and the church were one, no matter what. He belonged to it and it to him. He was the church. It took his death, my loss of him in this life, for me to be so sure.

And I am. Victor's greatest legacy to me is my love of the church. It belongs to me and I to it. I am the church. When she breaks my heart or makes me rage, I love her. "How to handle a woman?" King Arthur sings rhetorically in *Camelot*. His answer will do here as well: "Love her. Simply love her. Love her."

When this is easy, it feels like heaven on earth. This is when the church is openhearted, generous, courageous in matters of justice and love. It is hard when the reverse is true. When the church seems to me to be small-minded, defensive, protective or stingy with love, I want

· · · · · ·

to run. Sometimes I yell and scream. Sometimes I petition and march. Sometimes I spend all my energy to hold still, counting seconds until I can get away. And I do get away. I stay away until I can find my love. Until I can say "I am the church" without clenching my teeth.

I always pray. "Stay, Minka," he said when we had mounted the cathedral's steps. Prayer gives me the way to stay. Victor's legacy has taught me that God has had to bear this a lot longer than I have. If God can stay, I can pray until I find my love. When I have no words, I turn to these:

> O God of unchangeable power and eternal light: Look favorably on your whole Church, that wonderful and sacred mystery; by the effectual working of your providence, carry out in tranquillity the plan of salvation; let the whole world see and know that things which were cast down are being raised up, and things which had grown old are being made new, and that all things are being brought to their perfection by him through whom all things were made, your Son Jesus Christ our Lord; who lives and reigns with you in the unity of the Holy Spirit, one God, for ever and ever. *Amen.* *

Had I not stayed, I would not know Victor's legacy of love. When I can hardly bear it, I linger on the word "mystery." Praying with clenched teeth doesn't bother me at all. I treasure the church as my grandfather's watch. I love her. Simply, love her.

---

* The Book of Common Prayer, 540.

. . . . . .

WE WERE DISCUSSING Christian "calling" in faculty Bible study. Han, Professor of the Hebrew Bible, had led us out. "Call negotiations" between God and whomever, he said, happened predictably. A short form looked like this:

"Hey, you."

"Who, me?"

"Yes, you."

"Oh, no. Not me."

"Yes, you. Do this."

Han's wonderful description called out everybody's stories. I listened to these, sharing the poignancy and the laughter that arose. For myself, I confess, I was thinking of Luke's story of Paul on the road to Damascus in Acts and how bratty and backwards my own "call" feels in comparison. I did not think I would share.

Lost in my own sheepish thoughts, I was stunned to hear my most elegant colleague describe his calling with the word "primitive." Indeed, we all stared at him, awaiting explanation. There was some silence. At last, he smiled. "My primitive sense of calling came from a foxhole," he said.

This silenced me completely. The danger and violence in this confession, the very idea of the foxhole overwhelmed me. I do not think of this as "primitive" at all, although I think I know what he means. I think of this as miraculous, how remarkable it is that God got there. God moving into a foxhole for the life of this man makes me want to scream for forgiveness for being bratty and backwards.

I have never been in such danger, in proximity to such violence. In comparison to millions of other lives, mine has been exceedingly comfortable. The horror of war and my col-

· · · · · ·

league's humility make me feel that my own story is very small. There is a story, a particular conversation with God that turned my mind and set me on my present path. I even remember what I was wearing. Next to a foxhole, it feels pathetic and like a shameful waste of God's time.

But I accept forgiveness. This is the point, of course. God is so big and so clever and so good at being God that it is okay. God calls us all in a myriad of ways. This is how God's world is the way it is.

I left Bible study that day without a word. Here, away from the foxhole, I can confess. I must admit that "Who, me?" took a long time to reach my lips. "Absolutely not," I had said to God. "You are barking up the wrong tree."

I was certain that I was in seminary for the adventure, not the vocation. When the word "call" arose, I pointed to everyone else there. "Here they are," I said to God. "They like this. Send them."

By the time I thought I could see the light at the end of the seminary tunnel, this was still the case. I had, however, begun to pray, to talk to God all the time. "This has been nice," I said to God one afternoon, wearing my pink parachute workout clothes. "I'll soon be on my way." I embarked on a list of good reasons why this was not my vocation, good reasons not to be in the church.

"My dear," God interrupted. "The church has been very good to you."

"I know," I replied. "I'm grateful, I really am. But I can hardly bear her history and there are other things I could be doing."

"My dear," I heard. "May I remind you of all her history you have not had to witness, not had to bear?"

I was overcome with sadness for God. All the disappointments, the injustices, the violence over the years. "How," I finally whispered, "do you stay?"

. . . . . .

There was silence.

Weak in my knees, I heard me say, "I'll stay if you stay."

There was a little more silence. Then, "I don't care what you wear."

"*They* do," I shrieked. "*They* have uniforms."

"Minka, I do not care what you wear."

Next to a foxhole, this is a humble call. It is, however, the only call I have. No road to Damascus here, just an embarrassing taking of divine time. And the learning of how much God has to do, how much God has had to bear. I have learned to pray for God.

"Red cowboy boots with uniforms?" I ask.

"Yes, you."

. . . . . .

In the late 1970s, I watched the purchase of a paper shredder facilitate an administrative downfall. Paper shredders were unusual, belonged to the world of shocking national political events. Earlier in the decade, paper shredders accompanied Watergate, Richard Nixon's resignation as President of the United States. Paper shredders signaled bad behavior, implied an admission of guilt.

I was part of an institution with hardly the magnitude of the governance of the United States. The administration of this institution was, however, the leadership of a body. Complaints about this leadership had surfaced regularly for several years, going nowhere, but when the paper shredder appeared, the complaints landed. The bad behavior and guilt associated with Watergate marked the beginning of this administration's end.

Events from the last two decades could be chronicled a variety of ways. Wars, unfortunate human business as usual, could be listed. The Berlin Wall and the Soviet Union count as stunning dissolutions. The Empire State Building in New York City, oh my, shines annually in lavender on Gay Pride Day. Then, there is technology.

In this time, I have a paper shredder. It is hardly a signal of bad behavior, guilt of any sort. My shredder is environmentally sound, ecologically correct. It even offers what the world calls "security." Shredding direct mail credit is protection from fraud.

Look how the times have changed. Only one generation, given that a generation is twenty years. Counting this way, we are the hundredth generation since Jesus was born. Jesus himself was the hundredth generation of the people of God. It is startling how much life can change in just one of these.

I cannot count how many sermons I have heard about not getting it right in our generation. These "bad news" sermons encourage human guilt and shame. I know there are accu-

· · · · · ·

sations to be made about human responsibility in every generation. I certainly believe Jesus walked so that every Christian generation might stand for the marginalized and disenfranchised in society. There is, however, a truth about time these "bad news" sermons do not tell.

Our very existence as the hundredth Christian generation and the two hundredth generation as God's people suggests that God is here for the long haul. We are called to be part of God's long haul, contributing what we can to the well-being of God's world. Guilt and shame hardly help. Righteous anger followed by communion and joy contribute to the making of human energy; guilt drains it away. Generation-wise, there is something egocentric to the "bad news" sermons. We are not the only generation God has. The picture of God's world we see in any given moment is the size of one colored stone in a mosaic we will never recognize.

There is another truth about time as well. Not only is it longer than our imaginations; it is shorter. A butterfly's generation is fleeting enough to take our breath away. We cherish illusions about time. Philo, writing in Jesus' century, calls us to the truth of the moment: "Today means boundless and inexhaustible eternity. Months and years and all periods of time are concepts of men, who gauge everything by number; but the true name of eternity is Today."[*]

I called my friend Eleanor when I had the shredder up and running, told her my shredder story from the last generation. "God is moving," she said, laughing. "See how incarnations come and go."

Environmentally sound, ecologically correct, "secure." Even more, with the delight of shredding, the tyranny of junk mail is gone. So go the "bad news" sermons. "Here," I say to the God who moves, "you can recycle this, too. "

---

[*] Stephen Mitchell, *Tao Te Ching*, HarperCollins Publishers Inc., 1988, 94.

· · · · · ·

LUKE HAS TAUGHT ME to be careful how and where I name the opposition. He is careful with this all the way through both Luke and Acts, from before Elizabeth's conception in the gospel to Paul's last words in Rome. Luke-Acts is a long story in two parts in which the Holy Spirit is the main character. Consistently, the author is precise about where evil is, how it moves, what it is called by name.

Oh, yes, this evangelist is a healer. There is language in this story that only physicians in the first century would know. In the gospel, God moves so powerfully through the Holy Spirit and Jesus that evil is put on hold for Jesus' ministry. (Luke 4:13) In this time, the twelve and seventy more are commissioned to preach, teach, heal. They are successful. Evil returns as Jesus turns to enter Jerusalem, is the first character named in Luke's passion. (22:3) This writer knows there is no ending to the story of God's Spirit in the world, so there is no ending to Acts. Likewise, Luke knows that once Jesus turns toward the cross, there is no ending to opposition in the world, either.

In Luke's version of the Lord's Prayer, we are not taught to say, "deliver us from evil." (11:2–4) Luke-Acts is the story of the Breath of God moving in each generation for health, through conception, through Jesus, through the followers of Jesus, in Jesus' name. Forever.

Luke has taught me to expect opposition, that it has many names and faces. Evil can be the liar, twister of truth. Evil can be the adversary, good at disguise. Evil can be the enemy, confusion, or darkness. Back in action when Jesus' ministry is complete, the opposition claims the heart of the betrayer, sifts Peter, breeds darkness at the foot of the cross. The awful behavior and resulting deaths of Ananias and Sapphira in Acts 5:1–11 should come, Luke-wise, as no surprise.

. . . . . .

Luke has taught me that I will be called to dance the opposition, that this goes with human territory. We can all, like Peter, be sifted. Internally, I tend to flinch and duck when evil is named around me. I seek to avoid this; I do not want, ever, to give the opposition any more power than it already has. In my world, in every way, I want to be the next chapter of Acts: a healer in Jesus' name.

I expect to have to tell the opposition to get behind me. Silently or aloud, I sometimes hear me say, "If this is the best the opposition can do, I am in pretty good shape." And I always have M.J.'s words. In addition to being beautiful and making beautiful music, M.J. could swish elegantly through the choir room and drop the odd brilliant comment. This is the one I use to put the opposition in its place, find my way to laughter: "Good," M.J. said, "is infinitely creative and resourceful. Evil knows a few cheap tricks and they always work."

Then, as is so often the case, there is great Ephesians advice. "The contest for us is not toward blood and flesh," this wise one says in 6:11–12. "The contest for us is rather toward the spiritual things of wickedness in the heavenly places." He offers us a new kind of military uniform: the full armor of truth, righteousness, peace, faith, salvation. In this armor, we are to stand.

Oh, yes. With all that I am and all that I have, to be the next chapter of Acts in Jesus' name: here I take my stand.

TRAVEL UNHINGES, unravels me. When I am on the road, I make assumptions that I do not make when I am at home. *Chez moi*, the French say for "at home with me." Amazingly, I worry about what people will think about my behavior—what I wear, say, do. The reverse is also true: I find myself thinking I know about other people by way of their dress, the way they act. The fact that I do not make these assumptions when I am in my own regular space suggests that I am not "with me" the same way when I travel.

This happens, I've decided, because I am literally unhinged from familiar space. Familiar spaces come with regular routines for behavior that make us feel secure. When the spaces and routines are gone, we literally become insecure. Instinctively, somehow, I change—make assumptions about others, worry about me. Unhinged, I unravel like yarn. "Yuck," I think. This appalls me.

I know that what other people think is their business, that there is absolutely no way to control it. I can do whatever I am willing to do in anticipation of others, but I am essentially doing this for myself. When the chips are in, other people are who they are, will think whatever they think.

Growing up in a small town where most everyone knew everyone else, and had for generations, taught me this first. I thought I could escape and ran for the city in hope of anonymity. As one of 7,999 other freshmen at the University of Minnesota, I soon discovered size made no difference at all. The first week of class, a woman who knew my mother recognized me crossing the street.

By the time I was raising babies in an Ohio village, I sat up and took notice. Living in small places where most everyone knew everyone else was my call. I began to work on not making assumptions about other people, to choose my stuff and let it go.

· · · · · ·

It's a good thing, too. Eleven years at General Theological Seminary were waiting in my wings, life on a New York City block with walls around it. Very beautiful, but still, life inside walls. If I could learn to be *chez moi* there, at home with myself and letting go what other people thought, I could do it anywhere.

I learned to take a breath after the kids went to school. I would assemble my life, creep down half the stairs to my apartment. I would stop and call in the angels. "We are about to go public," I would whisper, "please guard my back." Often, I would find myself humming, "whatever will be, will be" as I walked out into the world.

It took me years to get the method down, call up faith. No wonder I feel appalled when I find myself worrying, making assumptions. I know better. I know I can't control others. About these others, I know that I really do not know.

It comes down to G. K. Chesterton's words, "We must learn to love life without ever trusting it." While I cannot recall where I read this, I know it is true. Travel unravel me tells me so.

And I do, love it, eventually. I also find that my habits change after I travel. I learn new ways to live. I learn me. I learn God and this remarkable creation anew, me in it. Eventually, I feel raveled, rehinged, *chez moi*, at home. Then, of course, I forget about travel unravel completely. Until I hit the road.

WHENEVER THE CHURCH makes me gag or rage uncontrollably, I remind myself that this is in my bones. This runs in my family, could be called "genetic drift." My mother's parents met in church. With this, they began their lifetime together, and, as the expression goes, sealed something of my fate as well.

The twentieth century was still in its first decade. My grandmother had been invited to what she called "a young people's weekend" in Kansas City. As I remember her telling it, this began with some sort of festivity on Friday evening. Saturday was spent outdoors with games and barbecue. There might even have been horses. A grand ball occurred on Saturday night. Sunday was spent in church, a picnic separating the morning and evening services.

I, of course, think of this as a Baptist Church. Where I grew up, only the Baptists had Sunday services twice. I could be wrong about this. I also imagine this weekend resembling the "young people's weekend" at Twelve Oaks in the beginning of *Gone With the Wind*. I could be wrong about this, too. The movies and my own experience have enabled these details to crawl into the story. Hoop skirts, surely, were long gone.

For the weekend, there was dance card after dance card. One of the young men in the party had been assigned to my grandmother as an escort. My grandfather was assigned as escort to the hostess.

"I was spent by Sunday," my grandmother said. "My disposition was gone. I was tired of this man assigned to my arm. I was tired of smiling. I was tired of picnics. By Sunday evening, I was tired of church. I had to go, of course. Where else was I going to go and how would I get there?"

The church, she said, was huge and full. "More of the same," she lamented, "more and more of the same. Until the altar call. And child, that alter call was the limit. The very limit."

. . . . . .

It wasn't the regular call to come up front and, for a first time ever, hand over your life to Jesus. It was much more general, issued to everyone. "The way it was put," she said, "if you didn't mash your way up there it meant you didn't like Jesus. Imagine."

She put her foot down, sat still. "I wasn't belligerent," she said a little defensively. "I just folded my nice little gloved hands in my lap, told Jesus I knew he knew better and stayed put."

She was listening to the crowds jostling at the front of the church when she heard someone whisper her name. "Psst, Mary Francis. Psst. Look at me."

"Child," she said, "it took all my courage to look. For all I knew, I had been wrong and Jesus himself was there."

She discovered that she and the hostess's escort were the only people in the church in their pews. "Jack Young!" she exclaimed.

"Shhh," said my grandfather-to-be, sliding over on the pew, motioning for her to lower her voice. "Mary Francis, will you be mine?"

From time to time, I hit the limit in the church. The very limit. Institutional life of all sorts can enrage me, make me gag. I lose my disposition. On good days, I can avoid being belligerent when this happens. On the best days, I fold my hands in my lap, tell Jesus I know he knows better and let go. This helps me stay. Then I add how glad I am not to have to wear gloves, how grateful I am for "genetic drift."

· · · · · ·

I WAS TELLING Laurie I had no idea what was going on in my life, where it was leading. "I haven't a clue," I moaned. "It feels like I ought to know what to do next, but I don't. I don't know at all. Would I recognize my own calling if I fell over it?"

"Upright," she said. "Stay upright."

"Okay," I answered, dubiously. "What exactly do you mean?"

"It's like jumping," she said. "The horse gathers itself and jumps up to you. If you lean forward and try to anticipate the jump, you force the horse to scramble. When the horse scrambles, it can fall. Riding instructors tell you to wait, be patient. They shout, 'Upright, upright, upright!' If you stay upright, the jump is there. Right there."

The way that horses jump up to their riders, hills rise to meet ski jumpers, too. Jumpers have a precise patience, it seems to me. They know partnership as well, with the animal, with creation. So, too, we do well when we give God the chance to move in creation and society, allow our lives to gather themselves up, rise to meet us.

This is, of course, one side of the coin. Sometimes proactive and programmatic is the only way to go if we want to become ourselves. Here, like decathlon athletes we must set goals, run to the clock, change tactics, push on no matter what. For these times in our lives, bookstores are full of manuals, I dare say. Self-help shelves offer a myriad of ways to prioritize, strategize, maximize.

For the "upright, upright, let the horse jump up to you" times of our lives, we more often need reminders. I keep these words as near as I keep Laurie's advice:

> Above all, trust in the slow work of God.
>
> We are, quite naturally,
>
> impatient in everything to reach the end

· · · · · ·

without delay.
We should like to skip
the intermediate stages.
We are impatient of being on
the way to something unknown,
something new,
and yet it is the law of all progress
that it is made by passing through
some stage of instability—
And that it may take a very long time.

And so I think it is with you.
Your ideas mature gradually—
let them grow,
let them shape themselves,
without undue haste.
Don't try to force them on,
as though you could be today
what time (that is to say, grace
and circumstances acting
on your good will)
Will make them tomorrow.

Only God could say what this new spirit
gradually forming within you will be.

. . . . . .

Give Our Lord the benefit of believing
that his hand is leading you,
and accept the anxiety of
feeling yourself in suspense and incomplete.[*]

Pierre Teilhard de Chardin speaks as a scientist as well as a theologian. He knows from the laboratory and observation that everything that grows must have "some stage of instability." Somehow, jumpers have trained themselves to accept what feels like instability before a jump. Scientists train for this precise patience, too.

I seek this training. I certainly want to give God the benefit of believing that I feel divinely led. The last thing I want to do is move in any way that makes God or God's world scramble and fall. "In suspense and incomplete" is under my pillow. For daylight hours, I'm mentally back in the saddle again: "Upright, stay upright."

---

[*] Pierre Teilhard de Chardin, "Trust in the Slow Work of God," *Faith @ Work* (Summer, 1997): 13.

. . . . . .

JUMPERS, FOR ME, are people who get on horses or skis. They are also uniforms for work, dresses that allow me to wear a clergy shirt and a petticoat underneath. Not in Belfast, however, where jumpers are sweaters; the dresses I wear with clergy shirts and petticoats are pinafores. In New York City, I do my banking at a teller window. In Niagara-on-the-Lake, Ontario, I get money at the wicket. I mash potatoes; Eleanor mashes the numbers on the phone when she dials a call.

In an introduction to New Testament class, I once rolled my eyes and said disparagingly, "That's like carrying coal to Newcastle." Blank faces looked back at me. I found myself talking about coal mining in England, how Newcastle was the last place that needed any more coal. "Hence the expression," I apologized, wondering if I got this from my mother.

"Hence the expression," Joe said to me said in the Edison Walthall Hotel in Jackson, Mississippi. "The door," he said. "Katy, bar the door."

"Katy, bar the what?" I had asked. I can't recall the story, just the point: close it off before anything else happens.

"Cut to the what?" Han asked me in a biblical field discussion.

"The chase," I said. Was this expression my mother's legacy as well? It comes from English fox hunting, for heaven's sake. If so, where did she get it?

"We do not have much fox hunting in Korea," Han said. "But I get the point: get to the point."

Here is the point: "It's only words, and words are all I have to take your heart away." The BeeGees sang this back in the days when paper shredders bespoke political guilt. Words are what God has to take our hearts away. Jesus is the Word made flesh, to take our hearts away.

· · · · · ·

Words are all we have to offer testimony of love, take our hearts away. This is also true: translation is sometimes necessary.

I was living at the Eden House in Key West, having my first big time sabbatical ever. This meant being totally lost. I was lost in space; never had I lived at home away from home for so long. I was working day and dream-time to become computer literate. I was trying valiantly to rewrite the Greek textbook I had used for years. Of course it was hurricane season, the one in which the names threatened to move through the entire alphabet. I smelled panic around every corner. When I learned to say to myself, "let the sun lead," and moved accordingly, things got better. Wonderful, even.

The day before I was to move home from home, friends of the owner arrived. They nodded to me as if they knew me, saying, "You're the translator, aren't you?"

It felt like my blackboard, so carefully filled, had been erased. I no longer had a clue who I was. I was so taken aback, I nodded in the affirmative.

Maybe so, I still think. Maybe we all are, one way or another, translators. Translation is moving words from one language into meaning in another, even when the language is shared. John's gospel holds before us the creative force of the Word, that "without the Word was not anything made that was made." (John 1:3) Words are serious business, life-giving or life-threatening they may be. When we do well, we do not have to eat them.

When all is said and done, they are all we have to take our hearts away. Hence this expression bears repeating: "I love you."

. . . . . .

THE WORD changed its way with me at dawn on a fifth Sunday in Lent, Year A. It traveled through me in new rhythms from unforeseen directions. I had arisen early to capture sermon thoughts into a text. The Word moved, I wrote, dawn became morning.

Once finished, I was sure John was right, "without the Word was not anything made that was made." I certainly had not made this. I hardly recognized the notes on the page. There was not a complete sentence in sight. Words from Lazarus's sisters had become a challenge and refrain, "Lord, if you had been here, my brother would not have died." (John 11:21,32) An old hymn from out of the blue had landed on these pages, "O Mary, don't you weep, don't you mourn."

Praying that whatever this was would be okay for the pulpit at the Cathedral of St. John the Divine, I dressed. "It hardly matters; I'll wear vestments," I thought, put on the old washed-too-many-times black dress. It was warm enough to wear the Irish cape to the train, up the cathedral steps.

Michael was singing the gospel when I arrived. "Ah, rehearsal," I thought to myself, walking down the south aisle. "Click, click, click" went my heels. It took me a moment to remember reality: Michael was the one of us who never needed to rehearse. He had a singing voice that could have been on Broadway. I picked up my pace.

Could this have been the day the time changed? Had I arrived to preach in the middle of the gospel?

Swept away with the Word, I had forgotten daylight saving time entirely. I was two football fields away from the pulpit. Mary's challenge bounced around the columns in Michael's lovely voice.

. . . . . .

The "click, click, click" of my heels began to sound like a drum roll. It would take too much time to take off these shoes, I couldn't arrive anywhere in stockinged-feet anyway. As fast as I could walk, I crossed behind the congregation. "Click, click, clicked" up the north aisle.

I pulled up at the foot of the mighty pulpit with, "Unbind him and let him go." (John 11:44) Separated by rows of the congregation and all the servers, I looked across at the dean. He stood below the pulpit between torchbearers as though he had been the appointed preacher all along.

"Do you want me to do this?" I mouthed silently to him. Neither of us moved another muscle.

"Yes, please," came the silent reply.

I took off the Irish cape as if it were a vestment I no longer needed, laid it over an empty seat. Michael descended the steps, the dean was escorted back to the celebrant's chair. I slid in between the torchbearers in the old washed-too-many-times black dress as if it had been foreordained from the beginning of time.

Jesus says we cannot expect to know times and seasons: "Of that day or that hour no one knows, not even the angels in heaven, nor the Son, but only the Father." (Mark 13:32) This makes me feel better, having learned that the power of the Word in my life can wash away time. The dean and I, thank God, still laugh. "Some choreography," he said. "The minute I heard those 'click, click, clicks,' I knew I was off the hook."

I have become more careful with clocks. When the fifth Sunday of Lent in each Lectionary A cycle rolls around every three years, I feel as if I am raised with Lazarus.

On every calendar I keep, St. Daylight Saving Time has become a movable feast.

· · · · · ·

Hosanna as a Child

· · · · · ·

ST. LUKE'S EPISCOPAL CHURCH in Darien, Connecticut, had invited me to speak on Palm Sunday. "Talk about why we do all these things on the same day," the Christian Education person said to me. "You know: processions, the long reading of the Passion, and all. Talk about what Palm Sunday means."

The glory of spring was in bloom all along the train ride. I was prepared to talk between the services, arrived for the early family one. The church was packed, particularly with children. "Has everyone in Fairfield County had a baby since I've been here?" I asked my friend Avery as we slid into the pew.

In the time since I had been there, they had also called a new rector. I was delighted to see that he was scheduled to preach "The Prone," the children's sermon. I would get to meet this man by way of the Word.

When the time came, he walked up and down the center aisle, passing out crosses to the children in the congregation. He had brought these tiny crosses back from Jerusalem. He talked about the trip, the importance of Palm Sunday. His basket seemed bottomless; I thought of loaves and fishes. There were no squawks when he returned to the front of the church; he must have had enough.

"Now," I recall him saying as he looked around the tightly packed, squirming congregation. "What is the worst thing I could do?"

Hands everywhere shot up. Squirming became tumultuous, seething. "Call on me! Call on me!" came from every corner of the church.

I leaned into Avery. "Do you know what it is?" I asked.

She shook her head. "But they seem to know," she said with a smile.

I marveled. I hadn't a clue.

· · · · · ·

The rector let tension rise. It was amazing. It felt like the reading of the Passion when the crowd calls, "Crucify him! Crucify him!" This was even more out-of-control. We adults say the words, hardly acting unruly while we do it. The children were thronging, demanding, surging. I thought of *The Lord of the Flies*, my all-time scary movie about kids. I wondered if Jesus had ever seen anything like this when he said, "Whoever does not receive the kingdom of God like a child shall not enter it." (Mark 10:15)

At last, the rector singled out one voice. "I know what the worst thing you could do is," this little one said on the edge of belligerence. "The worst thing you could do is take it back. That's the worst thing you could do!"

The room exploded with affirmation, "That's right! That's the worst thing you could do!" Children were standing and pointing and shouting in agreement everywhere.

The rector let this happen, too. "Yeah! That's the worst thing you could do!" bounced from the walls, climbed into every corner of the room. Finally, he signaled for quiet. He waited until it was very, very still. Then, he nodded. "That's right," he said. "That's the worst thing I could do."

"That's the point," he said. "On Palm Sunday, Jesus turns to give his life for us. He never takes it back." You could have heard a pin drop.

"Good God," I whispered to Avery. "They knew. And he knew they knew."

For a split second, I wanted to crawl out of the church on my hands and knees, all the way to the train. What else to say?

In communion, I came to my senses and knew: "Hosanna!" As a child.

· · · · · ·

As MULTIPLE SCLEROSIS claimed Marietta's body, the parishioners at Christ Church in Toms River, New Jersey, made sure she could share her soul. The calling committee scheduled its meetings with access, in time and in space. She prepared the children for first communion. When I wonder how to receive the kingdom of God as a child, Marietta's outstretched arms remain the picture of what Jesus means.

With the exception of the presentation of Jesus in the temple in Luke 2:22–52, our stories of Jesus are about the man, not the child. Kids rarely turn up in the gospel traditions at all. Jesus' teaching is with adults, about adult issues. In this teaching, he offers nothing less than God's kingdom, God's gift of life in creation. Jesus insists that this "kingdom" has drawn near, God's ways upon earth. Receiving this gift is teaching for adults, an adult issue. How startling it is when Jesus turns, implies that this will not work if we do it as adults. We may only receive the kingdom of God like a child.

In the story, Jesus does not explain what he means. "Like a child" is a metaphor, an image. Each one who hears these words must interpret them. We must find a way to picture this.

Marietta and I had met to discuss children, the Bible, and first communions before my adult education class. "I rarely get to drive," I told her, more than happy to be asked to bring her wheelchair around the house. She drove herself to the car. She positioned the chair so she could move herself from one into the other. We were in a rush. When she tried to hoist herself it didn't work.

"Wouldn't it be easier if I lifted you?" I asked.

"Are you strong enough?" she sweetly challenged.

"Marietta," I shot back with a smile. "I am the daughter of a professional athlete and my father's oldest son."

· · · · · ·

I leaned down. She stretched out her arms upwards toward me, palms to the sky. All the words in the world died in my throat, tears rushed to my eyes. Marietta's arms spoke trust, faith, love. These arms were both broken and strong. Her hands were not grasping. Nothing was held back here, nothing at all. "Willing," these arms said, "to put my life into your hands."

One of the words that society uses for Marietta's frailty is "disabled." We all are, one way or another. "Disabled" goes with human territory, being an adult. On earth, we will always live outside the Garden of Eden. We mean to love and we wound. We take what is not freely offered. We manipulate. We hold back little bits of love or little bits of money or little bits of time and keep it in secret. Like Peter, we mean well. We do not mean to deny Jesus' offer of God's kingdom on earth, but we do.

When we remember to stretch out our arms, willing to place our lives in God's hands, we have a chance to enter the kingdom of God like a child. All we must do is receive: receive God's love, receive God's assured forgiveness. I want to receive God's gift of life on earth like Marietta's outstretched arms: willing to put my life into God's hands, holding nothing back at all. I want to receive life like a child with truth, faith, love. Picture this: as open as the sky.

· · · · · ·

What If?

· · · · · ·

WHAT IF someone I love is or was or will be somehow, somewhere, someone who challenges my love? What if I cannot love someone I love for who they are or who they were or who they will become? What if I cannot love someone I love?

What does this mean about my love? That my love only dwells in certain places? That my love is insincere, here and there? That I have rules for my love to follow?

Does this mean that my love does end? That it is not patient, is not kind? That my love does not believe all things, bear all things, hope or endure all things?

What does this mean about my love if I cannot love someone I love because I love someone who loves another way? Because the love the someone I love makes is sometimes different than my own? Because the love the someone I love makes is another way, another truth?

What if the love someone I love makes gets a name in my society—a name to set it apart, set it aside, this way to love, this truth, this life? A name to identify, a political name for just this kind of love?

What does this mean about my world? Does this way to love exclude someone I love from my Body of Christ? My chosen race, royal priesthood, political office, military service, teacher of children, exclude from once you were no people, now you are God's people?

What does this mean about my world, my society, my government, my church if I cannot love someone I love because the love the someone I love makes is another way, another truth?

If there is "what if," am I not to wonder first about my love, the God I love, the world in which I walk? Am I not to ask how the idea of how love is made is made? Am I not to wonder why I wonder at all—what if, what if someone I love is anything at all? Am I not

· · · · · ·

to wonder why my society assigns a name to set apart this love, set aside this way for love, this truth?

Might I just as well wonder, what if Jesus had said "except?"

"The kingdom of God is at hand, except for you who make love this way."

"Love your neighbor as yourself, except this way."

"For God so loved the world, except..."

Might I just as well wonder, what if Paul had said "except?"

"There is nothing that can separate us from the love of God in Christ Jesus except this way to love."

"There is neither Jew nor Greek, slave nor free, male and female, we are one in Christ Jesus except if you love this way."

"For freedom Christ has set you free, except..."

What if? If Jesus or Paul had said "except," it would be so clear. My little society in my little nation in my little time would be right to set apart one kind of love, one way, one truth. Were this so very clear, I would be right to wonder: what if someone I love is gay? I would know love can be legislated, it does end. I would know my love doesn't have to bear all things, believe all things, hope all things, endure all things. If the cross or Christian freedom said "except" I would know this love was someone else's problem, not mine. But they don't.

So, what if? What if God—love divine, all loves excelling—did not create it all?

. . . . . .

MY DAUGHTER was recounting a story from her ministry as bartender. "He asked me how he could be so lonely in the middle of so many people. When I answered," she said, "I sounded like you."

"How so?" I asked.

"I said I thought it was the right question."

So it is, the right question. Being alone is the underside of incarnation, a built-in human contradiction to our social selves. Sometimes, this is lonely. Sometimes, not.

We come from communion into incarnation. We are conceived in community, out of some sort of union. Through birth, we arrive in what we call "life." Our parents are this community, but not the only one from which we are born. Generations and generations stand behind each one of them. We are born of all our people's ways. And then, God alone knows, this all happens in ways we no longer remember as we grow.

I am not the only one who has heard the story of the toddler's reminder of this human reality. How the little one's voice arrives into the midst of adult conversation. "Baby, wake up," the child says over the intercom monitor in the baby's room. "Baby, wake up and talk to me. I need help to remember. I'm beginning to forget about God."

In ways we no longer recall, we are conceived in communion and arrive through birth, willing to go it alone. Most of the rest of us are the rule here. Twins and other multiple births are the exceptions, continuing in life never quite alone. There is tension built into this birth, the yearning to be in community, the yearning to be alone. Apparent contradictions arise from the tension. We yearn for companionship, communion. We can also be "so lonely in the middle of so many people." We can cherish our own company, "alone."

What a friend we have in Jesus for this. The Gospels give us a way we can recognize. He comes into birth from community. Alone, he is baptized; alone, he begins in the wilderness. His walk is in communion, twelve to follow, women in attendance, crowds everywhere. He stops for everyone. From time to time, he also takes himself away—to a mountain, to a boat, to a "lonely place." He feeds himself with quality solitary time. He returns to play, to preach, to heal, to teach, to make love all the way to the cross. He seems to move effortlessly between alone and in communion in these stories. How does he do it?

My guess is that he is aware of being aware. From the baptism forward, he expects God to be there, expects power to come from prayer. One difference between Jesus and us, as far as I can see, is that his faith never wavers.

He must be forever watching himself. I imagine questions like these: Am I tired? Do I need time out? Why does this "party" feel like "work"? Why do I feel so lonely in the middle of all these people?

He seems to be forever checking in with God. He does not seem to care what others think. He seems to trust his own rhythms. He seems to take one day at a time. He seems to be his own best friend.

For life, alone and in communion, this may be the whole ball game.

. . . . . .

I HAD GONE, as the song from *Oklahoma!* goes, just about as far as I could go. When I agreed to go for the doctorate I had stepped out, so to speak, into wind, on water and waves. Colleagues and friends convinced me that this was a once-in-a-lifetime opportunity. They had faith that I could do it. "Try it" words of encouragement came from all corners. Dick Norris's words suggested to me that this was the only way I would know. "The Th.D. is an end in itself, not a means to an end," he said.

I had not yet learned how to say "yes" unless there was a good reason to say "no." Nor had I learned how to gain courage from the future negative, to ask myself if I had any reason to think I would regret not doing this. Seminary had been a surprise in itself. "Scholar" was not a word that had ever occurred to me. I stepped out on the faith of others, ready to "try it."

Step by step, I walked. I memorized the Greek moods in which Aristotle thought. I turned up for Evensong in the chapel. I memorized backwards in Hebrew. I turned up for Eucharist. I memorized the little bits of Aramaic we still have that lead us back to Jesus' own words. Step by step. "This is what I do," I would whisper to myself when panic clutched my heart in the night. The deadlines and step-by-step led me forward.

One day, I woke up in the middle of my life with the course work complete. I was certified—sometimes strongly and sometimes by the skin of my teeth—in all the languages but one-third of German. I was resigned about this one-third of German: I would take it and fail it in public until I passed it. This was discouraging and humiliating, but I could do it. I had everything I needed and I knew it: a strong body, the power of the Holy Spirit, good friends.

· · · · · ·

The realization of impending comprehensive exams made me think and I began to sink. Panic ruined my appetite and my dreams. I found myself bursting into tears in public. Desperate, I took to the city streets. I walked, step by step, block by block, mile by mile. I drank a million cappuccinos at the Cornelia Street Cafe, filled pages of journals with my fear. "God help me," I prayed silently and aloud.

Where was I when I finally figured out what to do? Somewhere in lower Manhattan is all I can remember. What remains indelible is the clear recollection of my own laughter, as public as the tears. "Oh my," I said to the Almighty, "I get it. This is in your imagination, not mine."

I revised all my prayers, step by step. "Thy kingdom come, thy will be done," I said as usual. Then, "And please, oh please, share with me your imagination. I cannot imagine how this can be done."

God evidently could, imagine. Step by step, block by block, mile by mile. Friends and colleagues supported me. Strangers came out of nowhere with fresh insight; cappuccinos sustained me. Through wind, on water and on wave, I crossed that sea.

"New things I now declare," God promised, "before they spring forth, I tell you of them." (Isaiah 42:9) Jesus took that promise, walked right out there on the waves. We may take that promise with Jesus' hand. These days, when I begin to think and start to sink, I hum music John Lennon made famous, step out on wind and wave. Imagine.

I MADE THE SEA CROSSING. The comprehensives went into an academic escrow account until I could pass the final third of the German exam. Week after week, I would walk to the library, do the exam. Week after week, my turgid translation would be inadequate. I was stuck.

My examiner was exceedingly kind. "I know you understand this language," he commiserated with me. He insisted that all I needed to do was relax. Week after week, I would walk home fighting back the tears. The people who loved me began to avoid making me tell them the bad news in public.

Victor could make this funny. I would call him each week with the rotten news. He would tease me out of the depths. These conversations became more and more outrageous. Each week, he lifted my heart with laughter.

In March, I took a weekend off, went to Miami to support a friend during ordination exams. Victor and I had lunch before he sent me off to the airport. We planned our fortieth birthday party for the coming autumn. In parting words, he sided with my German examiner. "You need sun and fun," he said, putting me on the train. "You'll relax. Come home in German!"

A visit with my brother-in-law was my Miami party favor. I told him about the comprehensives sea crossing while we stood in line to pick up buckets of barbecue. I lamented the pesky German translation. I described the walk of shame in every humiliating and frustrating detail. "How do you do all this?" he asked.

I didn't miss a beat. "I have everything I need: a strong body, the power of the Holy Spirit, the love of Victor Schramm," I confessed with laughter.

Victor was hit by a truck and killed within twenty-four hours of my return. His buoyant "Come home in German!" lingers with my last sight of his face.

· · · · · ·

The news came as we were dressing for chapel. My Hebrew professor held me close as he told me. In shock, I took off my vestments, walked to the door. My advisor reached out for me. "Where do you think you are going?" Barbara asked.

I stared at her, shook my head. I hadn't a clue. I was just going, robotlike.

"Come," she said, leading me back to the closet with my vestments. She opened the door, held out my cassock. "It's okay to want to run and hide. This is human animal instinct. But we are more than human animals here. We are the church."

She slipped the cassock over my head, handed me the surplice, adjusted my academic hood. "You belong here tonight, in the church," she said. "We are the Body of Christ."

I stared at her, robotlike. "We are now going to get in line," she said. "I would suggest that you get out those awful John Lennon sunglasses you wear. I think you will need them in church tonight."

Robotlike, I began to live without Victor in this world, wearing the awful John Lennon sunglasses he bought for me. Robotlike, I turned up for the German exam as usual. Robotlike, I sat to do the translation. Robotlike, I waited for the examiner to read my paper. I was beyond "relaxed." Robotlike, I passed.

Can there be laughter in heaven between departure and requiem? For the first time all week, my own laughter arose. I had certainly "come home in German." I put on those awful John Lennon sunglasses, imagined Victor's laughter mingled with my own. "Come," I whispered Barbara's words. "We are the church."

. . . . . .

R . S . V . P .

· · · · · ·

I WAS ON MY WAY HOME from a conference on "hospitality," the fifth one in a series of as many years. All week, I had heard us described as hosts: good hosts, look-how-these-people-have-their-backs-to-strangers-at-the-coffee-hour hosts. I had even learned that bad hosts are second only to evil in Dante's *Hell*. Out the airplane window, Pittsburgh was covered with snow. I had a single thought, tipped the Diet Coke right into my lap: "No one is host but God alone; we break this host to make communion."

I pressed the button for help.

"Are you all right?" the flight attendant asked, mopping up.

"I had a shocking thought," I apologized. "It made me clumsy."

I silently offered my gratitude to God, so glad that these words had not arrived on land. I was happy to take the soft drink in my lap. The conference had been wonderful. These words carried another truth.

Airborne, the Gospels were in my face. I could hear Jesus: "Why do you call me good? No one is good but God alone." (Mark 10:18) Airborne, I realized that Jesus was always the guest. No one is host in these stories but God alone.

Jesus is guest at everyone's table: women, tax collectors, Pharisees. He is guest when he heals in the homes of friends and strangers. He is guest of God's power to heal, he says so to the woman who touches his robe. (Mark 5:34) He is society's guest on the cross. His body lies as guest in a fresh grave. He even instructs: "Do not sit down at the place of honor in case someone more distinguished than you has been invited by your host." (Luke 14:8) And on the night he was betrayed, he took the cup and said, "I am among you as one who serves." (Luke 22:27)

· · · · · ·

No one is host but God alone. His mother knew this when she said, "Let it be to me according to your word." (Luke 1:38) She receives Gabriel as guest, conception as guest of the Holy Spirit.

We each come into life as a mother's guest. Breath upon breath, we bear God's Holy Spirit upon our spirit, God's Holy Breath upon our very own. Conceived as guest, we walk as God's guest with every breath we take. In communion, we invite in the name of the one host. We break this host to make communion; this is the banquet, this is the feast. No one is host but God alone.

To be guest of life turns everything upside down. Nothing is mine anymore: not my breath, my communion, not my faculty table, my ordination, my children, my city, my country, my world. In society and with the stars, no one is host but God alone.

All our talk of being good hosts, being hospitable is so embarrassing in the face of this truth. Whatever are we to do?

Let embarrassed be, first of all. To be God's guest, we get to be human, and embarrassed goes with human territory. Then, to be God's guest we are called to accept the forgiveness guaranteed by the cross of Christ. Frail and forgiven as God's guests, then we can step out in hospitality in the name of the one host and invite the world: to eat, to sleep in warmth, to learn to read, to disarm, to dance, to take the death by which we only know life for laughter and for love.

For this all, the fifth conference in a row on hospitality began with wonderful words. "The second hardest thing we do," said the Bishop of Minnesota, "is create and maintain a life of prayer. The first hardest thing we do is to be the Body of Christ."

To be this body, we are invited. So, too, to be the guest.

. . . . . .

. . . . . .

BASEBALL IS MY GREAT LOVE. My father played it, I grew up in it. I can even remember the young Roger Maris when he played for the Kansas City Athletics. This is a by-product of being my father's oldest son, something I admit when I am asked. I am rarely asked. But it is not graceful, elegant baseball that identifies my ministry. It is hockey. About hockey and prayer, I am asked.

"You are the one who prays for hockey at the cathedral?" the man asked me on the Number Six subway train. "I recognized the petticoat." Along with red cowboy boots, a flounce of lace below the hem of a dress has become my clergy uniform.

"I am," I answered. I braced myself for whatever was coming next. Harry Truman said it and I know it's true: "We can never tell what is in store for us."[*]

"I want to thank you," he said. "I had pretty much bullied my child into church a couple of weeks ago. When there were hockey prayers, the look on this kid's face was wonderful. I now have a child who is willing to come to church."

He touched my arm, turned to get off the train.

Silently, I thanked God. I laughed out loud. "We can never tell," indeed.

"What's on the list?" the Dean of the Cathedral would ask just before the big Sunday morning Eucharist. Were I to lead the prayers, I would write it all down. These names and occasions of the day would precede "Beloved, bid your intercessions..."

One autumn Sunday morning, the sound man adjusted the portable microphone on my vestments as the dean called for the list.

---

[*] David McCullough, *Truman*, Simon & Schuster, New York, 1992. Frontispiece.

. . . . . .

"You're all set," the sound man said. He stepped back and smiled. "Could we pray for a hockey season?"

"What do you mean?" I asked.

"There's a strike," he said. "We are losing the hockey season. Could we pray for a season?"

"I don't know why not," I said. I looked at the dean and asked.

"I don't know why not," he said.

Laughter rippled in the congregation with the prayers. Unwiring me later, the sound man thanked me. "Thank the dean," I said. He then told me of his family hockey tradition, generations of New York Rangers' fans. "My grandfather took my father to Madison Square Garden," he said. "When I was five, my father took me."

There were the odd hockey prayers long after the sound man had taken another job. I began to follow the hockey season, tucked in for Rangers' games with my needlepoint. Enthralled, I remembered meeting hockey in college in Minnesota. I cherished the ice, the speed, the direct hits.

I am a hockey regular now, admit it when I am asked. "How can you bear the violence?" I am always asked as well. I admit that I can't. When the violence erupts, I attend to the needlework on my lap. I do not like violence anywhere in my world. Given that I cannot make it go away, I prefer facing it in the game to facing it in war. Then, given the indirect hits of our political lives, I must admit that I find direct hits refreshing.

"We can never tell what is in store for us," indeed. This is also true: the time comes when we have gone as far as we can go. Hockey prayers drifted away after New Jersey made the Stanley Cup playoffs. "You are on your own here," I said to the congregation. "There is no way I can pray for a team with the opposition in its name. Beloved, bid your intercessions..."

. . . . . .

THE ATMOSPHERIC CONDITIONS of my growing up with baseball were, I must confess, fiercely anti-Yankees. This was Kansas City, where "they've gone about as far as they can go," Harry Truman country. It was always fiercely anti-New York Yankees.

The New York Yankees ruled the baseball world. Who didn't love Joe DiMaggio? Mickey Mantle was the home run star. Yogi Berra starred behind home plate. World Series titles reigned in the Bronx, rained on everyone else's parade.

Charley Finley's Athletics franchise had gone, for the time being, about as far west as it could go. Perched on the Missouri River, the A's seemed to function like a Yankees' farm team. Our good players went east. We lost our hearts with Roger Maris's departure, then had to watch him suffer as he bested Mantle's records. Celebrating every Yankees' loss went with my childhood like grits with scrambled eggs.

God does the choreography, so of course I moved to New York. Of course, my childhood "principles" were in my face. Did I go to Yankees games? Of course not.

Not that there was time. I went to seminary, took the kids to school, read history, took Girl Scout cookie orders. Being a student and a mother took precedence to being my father's oldest son. I let baseball go.

Time went, so did the kids. My love of baseball drifted back to the top, like cream in whole milk. The Yankees and my childhood "principles" were in my face. I had been "converted," please, and I knew it.

This is the way God and creation move, turning, turning. Winter converts into spring, time and space and all contexts convert as well. So do our ideas, our priorities, our "principles." I am now old enough to have seen myself step up to the unimaginable, step off where I said I would always stand. These days, I will admit that I only hold one "principle" that

· · · · · ·

cannot under any circumstances be challenged: "Christ has died. Christ is risen. Christ will come again."*

Long ago I smiled, said to my father in the heavenly reaches, "This is my city, this is my team." I am now in this city a quarter of a century. If the Yankees win one more World Series title, they will hold one for each of my New York City years.

The last two World Series wins for the Yankees have been different than the ones I watched as a child. There have been no stars like Mantle and Maris. The 1998 World Series title belonged to the Yankees as a team.

There are words about this season that take my breath away. Had my childhood "principles" not already been converted, these words would do it: "If they ask who was our star, give them twenty-five names. If you forget our names, just say 'We were the Yankees.'"

These words describe more than a team; they describe a body. There would be no body without the parts, of course. The parts are essential. But when each part plays for both itself and the whole, the body becomes more than the sum of its parts. This is what the Apostle Paul is trying to teach to the Corinthians, what Paul's disciple writes in the next generation to the Ephesians. We each matter. What matters even more is that somehow, as the church wherever we are, we are more than the sum of our parts.

I pray these words for the church: "If they ask who was our star, give them all of our names. If you forget our names, just say, 'We were the Body of Christ.'"

---

* The Book of Common Prayer, 363.

. . . . . .

PROFESSIONAL ATHLETES can always be traded. Sometimes, they are up for grabs for the making of expansion teams. How interesting it would be if we in the church, the Body of Christ, were subject to such conditions.

Pitchers, quarterbacks, right-wingers, point guards: they are always traded in their role. Wherever they go, they play the same part. We could do the same: trade bishops, deacons, ministers of all sorts, inside the denomination or to another one. We could trade congregational power pieces in our towns, send a Lutheran educator over to the Methodists. We could trade faculty members by fields in theological education, send a Baptist Church historian to a United Church of Christ seminary. In the Episcopal Church, we could do diocesan trades of all sorts. We could even assemble a denominational expansion diocese. Our Christian baptisms make us members of this Body of Christ. We could take our baptisms and our roles, lay and ordained, on the road.

In the years in which I let baseball go, the rules in the American League were converted. When I returned to the sport, pitchers in the American League no longer batted for themselves; "designated hitters" took their place at the plate. When the World Series rolls around these days, American League pitchers can look very foolish at the plate on National League ballfields. So could I, I think, were I traded to a Presbyterian seminary. Were it my call to be deacon and educator in an expansion diocese, I would have to practice. I would have to do a lot of work before I stepped up to the plate. I would bring my baptism and my experience to the position. There would be much about my part that would be the same. Much about my role, however, would change.

Parts of the body function in roles, play them. These roles can change, even when the position or the office remains constant. In the eight years I was at the Cathedral of St. John

· · · · · ·

the Divine, I was always deacon and educator. Inside this position, I moved from working with the Bible and sculptors to writing on environmental theology to praying for everything under the sun. The same is true for my years at New York Theological Seminary. Always professor, I have led committees and simply sat on them, chaired the faculty and not. In each of these positions, I have been able to witness the completion of call, the eventual realization of a new one. Watching calls come and go and changing roles can be extremely unsettling. To get through "what am I doing here?" times, I have taken it to lunch and taken it to prayer. Trading and expanding calls is hard enough. At least I haven't been traded to another team.

I work to remember that no one, rolewise, is indispensable but Jesus. And that his part has been played; we do not get it. I must also work to remember that it is my baptism that signs and seals me forever, not my position anywhere. I want to be, in whatever the role of the moment may be, the Body of Christ. For this, I treasure words from the movie *Star Trek IV* that go something like this: "Sometimes the one sacrifices for the good of the many. Sometimes, the many sacrifice for the good of the one."

When I am blessed, my baptism feels like solid ground. This is when I always remember that I am grateful that I'm not an American League pitcher, suddenly traded to a team where I have to learn to bat.

· · · · · ·

Bodies, no matter how well the parts play their roles, do not work very well without a head. This is Paul's point to the Corinthians: he wants them to remember that only Christ gets this part. This is a bottom line Christian truth, no matter the society, the role. What is also true is that, in society, bodies of all sorts need human leadership. The trick here is to remember that leadership roles, like times and seasons, come and go.

In China, at about the same time that God spoke by way of Second Isaiah in the land of Persia, more than five hundred years before Jesus, Lao Tzu wrote a manual for leadership. Lao Tzu named three "treasures" for leadership: compassion, moderation, daring not to be first in the world.[*] I have put these under my pillow. They help me remember that no matter my responsibility at the time, Christ is the head of my body, the head of every Christian body everywhere.

Even when I've got my body and my baptism straight, however, my person and my role can conflict. This, like human bodies needing leadership, goes with human territory. The conflict between person and role can happen many ways: insecurity can make us greedy, fear can drive us toward ego fulfillment, love can confuse us.

The greatest of these is love. The power of love is a basic ingredient of creation and the cosmos, a binding force among all bodies. Love is no respecter of our roles. The Greek mythological Cupid, replete with bow and arrows, bespeaks love's ability to strike at will. And we do "fall" in it, love. Love can make us lose our minds.

For a body to stand in society, its members and its head need to keep their minds. When insecurity, fear and love strike, we somehow have to balance who we are as a person, who we are in our role.

---

[*] R. L. Wing, *The Tao of Power*, Doubleday & Co., Inc., Garden City, 67.

My friend Murphy talks about this in terms of space, envisioning a place to walk between person and role. We were talking about leadership of the congregation and personal friendships. "I must reserve the space I need in order to lead," she said. I recognize this as teacher in the classroom, deacon in the community. I also know how wonderful it is when I can let this space go. I feel blissful freedom when the context or the responsibility has changed. When the space for leadership is no longer necessary, I am free to laugh and love as one of two, one among many.

When my personal self-interest conflicts with my role as leader, I work to honor the role first, make self-interest wait. If my self-interest is real and true, it can wait. If it is a momentary cosmic attempt to knock me off the track, it will not be there later. There are times when I struggle, of course. A seventy-two hour watch is always a good place to begin.

This is as close to a guiding "principle" for leadership as I get. I have learned it the hard way, of course. I have moved too quickly in conflicts of role and self-interest, sacrificed my role for my own needs. My authority as leader of the body has usually paid the price.

Once this price was worth it. I was struck by angelic love that I would not have missed for the world. Exceptions, as the saying goes, prove the rule. I only have one rule with no exceptions. When it falls to me to me to be leader, I hold on to Christ, do my best to head off trouble.

HERE IS PIERRE TEILHARD DE CHARDIN, priest and scientist: "Truth lies in seeing that everything gives way in the direction, and under the influence, of beauty and goodness. That is the inner face of evolution..."* Speaking of prices to pay, his was very high. The church could not bear his truth, would not allow him to speak it as priest.

I have discovered that when I insist that my self-interests take second place to my role as leader, they evolve as well. When my own needs are still there—long after seventy-two hours have passed, when I am no longer leader—they have been converted. They evolve more clearly when they have lived through time and space. Sometimes, I am even able to see how beauty and goodness have polished them.

Scientifically and religiously, Teilhard saw beauty and goodness in the way rocks, fish and humankind became themselves. He knew beauty and goodness in words, communion, human relationships. I would take his "inner face of evolution" one step further. I would say, "the inner face of God."

I hear his claim for all creation in the ancient Christian words of the Exsultet, Easter Vigil words:

> How holy is this night, when wickedness is put to flight, and sin is washed away. It restores innocence to the fallen, and joy to those who mourn. It casts out pride and hatred, and brings peace and concord.
>
> How blessed is this night, when earth and heaven are joined and [humanity] is reconciled to God.

---

* Nicole Mones, *Lost in Translation*, Delacorte Press, Bantam Doubleday Dell Publishing Group, Inc., New York, 1998, 153.

We get a glimpse of wholeness, of all things brought to their perfection in the Easter Vigil. Blessed indeed is this one night each year when the inner face of God is before our very eyes. What we think separate is joined. What we think fractured is whole. What we think low moves to heights. What we think far off is near. What we think irreconcilable is reconciled to God.

The Exsultet words bespeak the same coherent, interdependent, creative universe that Teilhard could see stone by stone. How blessed is the glimpse, inner face of evolution, inner face of God.

Creation herself attends the Vigil. It is no accident that the Vigil is to be held in the dark, after sunset on Holy Saturday and before sunrise of Easter morning. The darkness is one of creation's basic ingredients, already in place when God begins to move in Genesis 1:1. There is a holy fire to be lit and struck in this darkness, the coming of light. There is water to be hallowed and blessed. There is oil for anointing, fruit of the vine for the making of communion.

Gathering together with creation in the darkness makes it easier to see the glimpse: all things, all things are being brought to their perfection in the direction, and under the influence, of beauty and goodness. We are reconciled. This is the inner face of evolution, this is the inner face of God.

"We have been baptized into a death like his," Paul says, "…so we too might walk in newness of life." (Romans 6:4) Glimpsing the inner face of perfection and reconciliation, beauty and goodness: this is the newness of life.

In full light, the fractured, the estranged and the fallen will be clear. This is evolution's outer face, business as usual, oldness of life. How blessed are we to keep vigil, this holy night.

. . . . . .

IT WAS A BIBLICAL REVIVAL of an Episcopal sort. I spent the weekend talking up Bible study: Friday with the officers of the church, Saturday morning with the women's groups, Saturday afternoon with the high school group. Bible study was the subject at dinner. I preached on Sunday morning, taught the adult Bible class after church.

It felt as if it had gone well. I had certainly changed my clothes often enough. The rector of this congregation—who had this brainstorm in the first place—seemed pleased. I even had an honorarium in my bag.

I did the Gospel of John for the adult class. There were good questions and insightful comments when I finished the lecture. Then, one man asked, "Do you believe that all that John says is true?"

I will forever be able to describe this man's body as he spoke. It was hard for him to form his words. Agony played in the lines on his face, the tightness of his shoulders. This was painful and it showed.

The attention of the fifty or so people in the room turned his way. The oxygen in the air disappeared. I wondered what was happening.

I inhaled deeply. "What exactly do you have in mind?" I asked.

"John 14:6," he shot back. "No one comes to the Father except through me."

"Ah," I said. I lined up New Testament colleagues behind me as the authorities. I discussed "the Johannine community." I talked about how John's community has been thrown out of the synagogue, how the story is defensive as a result.

I did my best to be entertaining. "The problem is one of higher math," I said. "To some members of this community, Jesus + the Father = One. To others, this is not only bad math, it is blasphemy." I worked hard to explain how the context and community behind literature sets its tone.

There was silence when I was done. I waited for him to speak, thinking that whoever he was, he certainly seemed to be respected by everyone in the room.

He sat with his arms on his knees, his head in his hands. Finally, he met my eyes. "Do you believe this?" he asked. "Do you believe that you can only get to God through Jesus?"

I took a breath, reminded myself that it never gets any harder than this. I thanked God that I had an airplane ticket and a check in my bag. Then I stepped out.

"No," I said, "I don't. The God I worship has been known by all kinds of names and in all sorts of traditions since before recorded time. I worship this God by way of the Christ. Others worship this God with other names, other paths."

Haltingly, he explained. With his head back in his hands, he told how his son had joined a non-Christian community. How he had worked to persuade the boy, kidnapped him to bring him home. How he had done all he could, had given up. "For five years," he said, "I have feared for his life on earth, his life in hell. I have been afraid for my own salvation. I have been afraid and ashamed to tell this to my friends. Are you telling me that I do not need to have this fear?"

"I am," I shot back. "The God we worship can sort this out."

Everyone in the room turned to this man, showered him with their love, their care. "Why didn't you tell us?" he was asked over and again.

I insisted that we pray to close. I needed to make my plane. In my last look from the door, he was smiling every time he said it, "I was afraid." This is, for me, revival.

. . . . . .

His Holiness the Dalai Lama and the plight of his people have captured my daughter's heart. The God we worship can sort this out.

As a result, we support Tibetans and work for a free Tibet whenever we can. The proceeds from delicious soups and dumplings at the Tibetan Kitchen go to this cause and I am happy for it. I gladly contribute to Martin Scorcese's dividends every time I watch or recommend his movie about the Dalai Lama, *Kundun*. Like my daughter, I have become a regular at Potala, the midtown Manhattan Tibetan shop. Their books, jewelry and butter lamps make wonderful gifts. I wear their shirts as clergy clothes. I often find something intriguing to read. Most of all, inside this shop there is always peace. I stop by Potala for just this: sight, sound, scent of peace.

The Apostle Paul coined the phrase, "the peace of God which passes all understanding," in Philippians 4:7. Volumes have been written for how this is true, how little we know of peace beyond not-war. A generation later, Christ is named as peace in Ephesians 2:14. This wonderful disciple of Paul's says Christ "has broken down the wall of hostility." I believe this definition, stand on it. In Potala, I can feel this, the absence of hostility, no dividing walls.

This strikes me as ironic. I am certain that God is working on the big picture, sorting it out. Still, I fiddle with this in my mind. I am stopping by Buddhism to feel my Christian faith. I have come to realize that this is sensory: in Potala, I can see, hear, smell peace.

Some of this is due to ancient Tibetan Buddhist practices, surely. Colorful woven fabrics and rugs are everywhere, the sound of chanting mingles with aroma of incense. This is nice, would be nice anywhere. What makes the difference for me here is that the beauty of sight, sound and smell is deeply grounded in compassion. Each Dalai Lama is the embodiment of compassion. Breathing, walking compassion in the world is every Dalai Lama's life. The depth of compassion in this tradition, accompanied by sight, sound and smell of beauty, brings me to peace.

I stand on the author of Ephesians' definition of peace. I am also walking with my friend Paul Gibson's definition of compassion, "a tenderness for the whole world." My tendency is to see injustice clearly, to struggle with rage. Having a tenderness for the whole world comes much harder to me.

Speaking of injustice, His Holiness the Fourteenth Dalai Lama, has lived most of his life in exile. It comforts me to read that he, too, has struggled with anger. In 1995, he spoke of meditation on compassion and emptiness:

> These two practices really did change my life. I began to understand something about the possibility of salvation, the permanent cessation of all negative emotions. Once you're convinced that salvation is possible, you work toward it steadily and your faith becomes much stronger. The more I concentrated on compassion in the late Sixties and late Seventies, the more patient I became, the less prone to anger. Anger still comes, but it's more like a lightning flash now, it doesn't last.[*]

We must find peace of some sort if we are to move to compassion. Compassion is necessary for healing of any kind to occur. I find it wondrous that His Holiness and the people of Tibet find compassion in such excruciating circumstances. And what a divine-design, their offer to me of the finding of peace.

I have been asked if my daughter is religious. A million dumplings and rewindings of *Kundun* later, I smile and shake my head. "She's spiritual," I say. The God I worship is sorting this out.

---

[*] Mary Craig, *Kundun*, Counterpoint, Washington, D.C. 1998, 288.

NEVER IN MY LIFE, I realize in these mid-life years, have I had a single inclination to scramble up cliffs or dive beneath the sea. Perhaps this is a by-product of growing up in middle America, on lush farmland between the Missouri and Mississippi Rivers. There were neither tides nor mountains to beckon me; I didn't notice their absence.

I did, however, notice other absences. When a fabulous Roman Catholic girl turned up in high school, I wondered where the rest of these people were. I went looking and they turned out to be right there under my nose. I discovered that Roman Catholic kids went to school out of town. Aware of invisible Roman Catholics, I went looking for Jewish people. They were not right there under my nose. I had to drive out of town to find them, to Harry Truman's library in the next county even to read about them. The absences I noticed were people, not mountains or seas.

I took my human life at sea level for granted for a very long time. Archaeology was my awakening. My field of study is dependent upon archaeology; we know who we are as Christians and Jews by digging for who we have been. I thrilled the first time I could physically touch a wall built in the Roman Empire. I followed Laurie to live on Mount Canaan and dig in Hazor one summer. We showered off dirt older than all of Judaism. I began to think about how earth buries our civilizations, treasures them, holds them for our rediscovery.

Michael Crichton's essays about his travels and Key West stole my heart in the same year. Suddenly, I began to take sea level seriously. I became fascinated with people who climbed astonishing heights, people who deep-sea dived. I learned about the disciplines and rhythms such adventure requires, how the human body uses oxygen, manages heights and depths. All I knew was the Apostle Paul's strong claim in Romans 8:38: "I am convinced that neither death nor life, nor angels nor rulers, nor powers, nor height nor depth, nor anything else in

· · · · · ·

all creation will be able to separate us from the love of God in Christ Jesus our Lord." I learned that height and depth without supplemental oxygen can separate us from this life on earth.

These days, I depend upon adventurers of all sorts for learning and life. I am digging in my soul, seeking to uncover myself. I snorkel dive into literature to understand something of the worlds that exist in the water that keeps us all alive. I climb heights in movie theaters to feel Mount Everest. I read *Outside* magazine. Literature, film and cable television offer me worlds, inside and out, I would never know otherwise.

Any way we can, we need to find ways to be reminded of who we really are. I am paraphrasing Crichton here, learning himself by travel in unfamiliar places. Any way we can, we need to find ourselves. David Brashears, willing to claim the term "iconoclast," says it outright: "The risk inherent in climbing such mountains carries its own reward, deep and abiding, because it provides as profound a sense of self-knowledge as anything else on earth."[*]

Happy to have my feet right here on earth, I no longer take sea level for granted. I hug the coastline and celebrate the oxygen-rich air that I breathe. Generations of Spragues have put their toes in the Atlantic Ocean at the edge of Long Beach Island and I am privileged to count myself among them.

---

[*] David Brashears, *High Exposure: An Enduring Passion for Everest and Unforgiving Places*, Simon & Schuster, New York, 1999, 304–305.

FAITHFULNESS is a day-to-day, lifetime endeavor. The routine stuff of our lives can distract us, big stuff can do the same. The minute we are distracted, faithlessness is ready to pounce. Even when our lives are going well, we can be distracted with thoughts like "When is the other shoe going to drop?" Faithfulness lies in remembering that this loving God does not "drop the other shoe." Faithfulness is certainty that even the losses in our lives are moving in the direction of goodness and beauty in God's divine-design. As the old song goes, God has the whole world in loving hands, whether we can see it or not. Faithfulness is the way we go forward. There is no way to go forward without stepping out on faith.

The best biblical story I know about distraction and faithlessness is Jesus walking on water. (Matthew 14:22–33) Having fed the multitude, he sends the disciples to the other side of the lake. He takes himself away to pray, to fill for faith.

When he returns, the disciples are floundering. Jesus, however, is at full strength. He walks through wind and wave to reassure them and terrifies them even more. Something of their faithfulness returns only when he speaks. It is Peter, of course, who is willing to step out on this faith, "Lord, if it is you, command me to come to you on the water."

Peter's faithfulness only lasts so long, so far. Peter can walk on water until he thinks about it. The minute he thinks about it, he sinks. There is nothing like a miracle for distraction. "You of little faith," says Jesus, "why did you doubt?"

We all doubt. We all can lose our balance in our lives, tumble into faithlessness that keeps us from going forward. We can wake up in the middle of our lives, wondering how we got where we are. It is easy to recognize Peter's distraction and panic in the story.

Ready to pounce, faithlessness brings a friend, the illusion that backwards is an option. In the story, going backwards is literally sinking to the depths of the sea. In our lives on dry

. . . . . .

land, our faithlessness can whisper the possibility that we can stop right where we are and resume our safe-and-secure lives.

If we have actually made a mistake and need to turn back, prayer will let us know. In the story, Peter is sure he's made a mistake, he does not pray. Most of the time, however, the terror is one of the opposition's cheap tricks. Prayer lets us know this as well, helps us remember that our whole universe is moving forward, that we are where we are supposed to be. Prayer helps us remember that God has us in loving hands.

My cousin Kathy has taught me to invoke sharks when I pray through my terror for faithfulness. Once, stunned with her courage and resilience, I blurted out the question, "How could you do that?"

"I used the movie *Annie Hall*," she confessed with laughter. "You know that place where he says that relationships are like sharks, that they have to keep moving forward or they will die? I decided I was a shark and I had to keep moving forward. That's all. I didn't want to die."

This has become my regular and least elegant of prayers. I invoke the power and direction of sharks. This least elegant of prayers keeps me walking on top of the water until I can find faithfulness: "Almighty and most merciful God, I do not think I want to be a dead shark here. Help me go forward, help me remember that the whole world is in your hands..."

IT FELL TO MILLS OMALY to be the first Episcopal priest from the Diocese of New York who had to walk into the bishop's office and say, "I have AIDS." His dying was a problem for the future. The problem of the moment was support for the rest of his living. Stepping out as a gay man was a noteworthy by-product.

The bishop and the diocese rose to the call. Mills was loved and cared for to the end. He loved and cared for others, too. "I have a new ministry," he said to me from his hospital bed, wonderment in his eyes. My eyes, too. Was this when I began to think of my life echoing Ephesians' words, "more than I can ask or imagine?" (Ephesians 3:20) In the year Mills brought us out into the AIDS epidemic, we all became more than we could imagine.

As he had lived, Mills went out in style—a Pontifical Mass of the Resurrection, all three bishops present. Family and friends prepared to converge at St. Luke's-in-the-Fields in Greenwich Village. The service would be in the school gymnasium, the church being rebuilt after a fire. It was to be a funeral to remember, a service worthy of rehearsal.

Chuck and I were glad to be asked to offer the prayers. Each of us and to do it together. He was my gift, more than I could ask or imagine, for doing the doctorate at General. He was smart and honest. My foibles never escaped him. He taught me new ways to dance. We shared laughter, such laughter. Healing laughter.

We needed it, this healing laughter. As if the pressures of graduate school were not enough, we were in the middle of a raging epidemic. We were, reasonably, terrified. In those early days of AIDS awareness, the Gay Men's Health Crisis was an infant institution. Newspapers would not print the stories, say the words. When Mills was first hospitalized, nurses would not touch him. God knows, we needed the healing laughter.

· · · · · ·

We dutifully turned up for rehearsal, along with the throngs who would do this elegant funeral. Crowded into the gym at St. Luke's to practice, it was solemn. Exceedingly solemn.

Bishops, readers, servers, psalmists were choreographed. Solemnly. At last, the master of ceremonies approached us. Solemnly, he knelt down by the chairs so we would be sure to hear him. "When the creed is finished," he instructed, "step up to the free-throw line to offer the prayers."

My eyes hit my boots. Until that moment, the solemnity held me. The devastation of loss was in my bones. The idea of stepping up to the free-throw line to pray, however, was the funniest thing I had heard in days. More than I could ask or imagine.

"Do not look at him," I said to myself. I could feel the laughter rising in my veins. I could feel Chuck's body tense, the air between us electric. I knew better than to meet his eyes. I knew that raucous laughter in this moment was inappropriate.

I ducked my head so I could not see Chuck, tucked my chin onto the top of my sternum. We rehearsed. "Is this all?" I asked. It was. Head down, I crept solemnly toward the door, could feel Chuck behind me.

Outside and without a word, we broke into a sprint. Safely away, we exploded with laughter like twin volcanoes. We rolled on the grass, tears flowing down our cheeks. "Praying from the free-throw line? Thank you, Mills," he said. Healing laughter.

"Thank you, Jesus," I replied. "More than I could ask or imagine."

· · · · · ·